ADD Rescue

Help Your Child Survive and Thrive With ADD

Dr. Leon Schofield

Licensed Clinical Psychologist

ISBN-13: 978-1544124377
ISBN-10: 1544124376

Library of Congress Control Number: 2017905399
CreateSpace Independent Publishing Platform, North Charleston, SC

DEDICATION

I dedicate this book to the many ADD children I have met over the past three decades. The courage and determination that ADD children and their parents have shown in facing and managing ADD issues has been inspiring. Without any easy or quick "cures," you have had to struggle and cope. You have helped me to listen and understand in my journey to fully appreciate the complexity of ADD. Thank you.

ACKNOWLEDGEMENTS

I am primarily indebted to my loving wife, Pat Schofield, for her months of reading, correcting and focusing this effort. As the voice of clarity, she has spared the reader much wandering in the literary wilderness. She has also been the voice of the parent reader, trying to make sense of this complicated and frustrating topic. She has worked diligently to get me to "say what you mean" with clarity and conviction. She has been the patient supporter who forfeited much time to this joint effort. She is the silent co-author. Thank you.

I am also extremely grateful for the efforts of Judy Marksteiner, who has been a staunch supporter of my writing efforts and an excellent scout, spotting spelling and grammatical errors invisible to these eyes. She has also been an able technical support person in the preparation of this manuscript for publication. I want to thank Teresa Miller as well for her assistance in reading and advising. Thanks are also extended to Judy Loose for her able assistance with cover design and for her help in preparing and formatting this manuscript for publication.

INTRODUCTION

After many years of evaluating and consulting with parents, doctors, teachers and counselors I have concluded that we are not yet doing as well as we should in our treatment of ADD. Some progress has been made over the last couple of decades. However, we are often still struggling to help many of our ADD children.

Reasons for often poor performance in diagnosing and treating ADD are many. They include:

- Different types of ADD require a variety of different treatment approaches.
- Reliance on history taking and rating scales in the diagnosing of ADD can be quite subjective.
- Medication as the primary treatment often has mixed results, especially with some types of ADD.
- ADD children often have a complex mix of emotional, behavioral and academic skill problems.
- Treatment approaches vary widely depending on the experience and skills of the doctors and counselors.
- Educational planning and supportive services vary greatly from school to school.
- Most importantly, ADD children are rarely involved in the evaluation of their ADD, treatment planning and educational planning.

In this book, I encourage parents to develop a collaborative approach to the management of ADD. ADD children will be asked to be very actively involved in their diagnostic evaluation, treatment planning and educational planning.

A collaborative approach involving your ADD child provides a wide range of benefits including:

- Greater ownership or acceptance of their ADD
- Better self-management of their ADD
- Greater resiliency in the face of setbacks and frustration
- Greater independence
- Improved coping skills
- Improved longer term success

The traditional approach to diagnose and treat ADD has been to assume that parents, teachers and doctors are the authorities. Adults assess the child and create treatment plans and educational plans that they believe will work well. The problem with this approach is that it leaves the child out of the diagnostic and treatment process. It presumes the ADD child is ill-equipped to contribute to this process. The traditional approach does not prepare your child to be more independent and self-managing. It also encourages either active or passive opposition by your child. At the other extreme, it may actually increase risks of your child becoming dependent upon accommodations and support.

The focus of this book is to offer a number of tips for parents to help their child learn to self-manage ADD more effectively. These tips have been gleaned from many years of diagnosing and treating ADD children and adults in my private practice. These tips offer alternative approaches that parents will find helpful. These tips have an underlying theme of bringing your child into the entire process of diagnosing and treating ADD. A collaborative effort with you and your child working together will produce greater short and long term benefits.

The collaborative approach is used in each chapter to discuss when and how your child can participate. You will find the writing style to be more relaxed and informal. The "reader" will interrupt the text to ask for clarification and examples, to offer a comment, and to provide a critique. The informal writing style is designed to feel like a consultation at my office, rather than an ADD lecture in a classroom. Each chapter will close with a question that summarizes key points in that chapter.

Before beginning, let's discuss some terms used in this book. The term "ADD" is used to refer to both types of ADD, hyperactive-impulsive and inattentive. Many tips offered here will be appropriate for both types of ADD. The terms "hyperactive ADD" and "inattentive ADD" will refer exclusively to children who present the symptoms associated with these subtypes, as defined by the AMA's guidelines. Often there will be some modifications of the tips offered to fit these subgroups.

You may be a parent at the early stages of identifying and treating ADD. Be sure to read as much as possible about ADD. This book will help you develop strategies that will work, but it is not intended to be a full treatise on ADD. You may be a parent who has worked with your child for many years with minimal success. This book will help you to break out of traditional methods of management and it will help you to view ADD in a very different way. It may open up new approaches to get on a positive track.

For further information about ADD I would invite readers to view my ADD website, **www.addexpert.net**.

Let's get started!

Dr. Leon Schofield

TABLE OF CONTENTS

Chapter 1: Make your child a collaborator

Suggestions are offered to help foster a collaborative role for your child in the diagnosis and management of ADD. Your child can take an active role in the diagnostic and treatment process which can improve the chances for compliance and for better self-management of ADD.

Chapter 2: Consider objective testing to diagnose ADD

Parents can learn to advocate effectively for their ADD child with objective testing data. Many schools can provide appropriate testing. If needed, parents can seek a private evaluation if they are not satisfied with the type or extent of the testing, or if they simply would like a second option.

Chapter 3: Seek help from school early

The usual "let's wait and see" approach by parents and school officials has great risk. Strategies are presented to help enlist school staff support.

Chapter 4: Know the limitations of medication

We seem to want every problem to be fixed by medication. This chapter helps parents to know what medication can do to help manage ADD and what it can't do. This chapter discusses how parents can seek medication trials with your child's doctor or with a specialist.

Chapter 5: Reward process, not product

ADD children often can't complete a task and therefore may not achieve standard rewards. Parents will learn to reward the attitudes and the behaviors that are necessary to complete the task. ADD children can learn to manage the necessary steps to keep them on task.

Chapter 6: Use humor

Humor helps your child reduce the chances of having a negative reaction with failure and frustration. Humor helps them stay open to various management options. Humor provides an opportunity for your child to stay connected with others. It can be used at all stages of evaluating and managing ADD.

Chapter 7: Use limited punishment

ADD children often provoke far more punishment than children without ADD. The reasons why punishments don't work well with ADD children are explored. Modifications of punishment procedures are suggested to help your child develop better coping skills with less conflict.

Chapter 8: Move and exercise

Movement is necessary for many ADD children. Suggestions are offered to help ADD children to move without distracting others. Exercise also helps ADD children to channel and direct their energy through physical activities outside of school.

Chapter 9: Self-talk, the secret weapon

Positive internal language or "self-talk" can have huge benefits for ADD children. Internal language can help manage both thought and emotion, as well as help to guide verbal and physical action. Internal language or self-talk can help children focus and problem solve. It is a form of "self-coaching."

Chapter 10: Improve communication and social skills

ADD children often have poor communication and social skills. This can create major problems at school and at home. Parents will learn to help their child by coaching them and by providing practice with a set of short "scripts" that can help with communication and social interactions.

Chapter 11: Build real self-esteem

Most ADD children have damaged self-esteem. Real self-esteem comes from self-acceptance – knowing your own limitations and advocating for yourself. Real self-esteem also comes from learning new and effective coping strategies and from developing new skills and talents.

Chapter 12: Help your child to manage blowups

Many ADD children react with significant emotionality to delay, frustration, roadblocks to their plans, or to criticism. This firestorm of excessive emotion is perplexing, frustrating and even frightening for parents and teachers. Some easy to learn interventions will reduce blowups.

Chapter 13: Parents, take care of yourselves

Parents and teachers are human. They can be worn down by the demands of an ADD child. Parents must learn to care for themselves in order to continue to help their child. Neglecting your own needs will not be helpful in the long run.

Chapter 14: Prepare your child for the future

ADD is lifelong. Your child must separate from the family and move into a productive adult life. In this chapter, advice is given to help parents guide their adolescent and young adult children to a more productive and successful future.

Chapter 1: Make Your Child a Collaborator

Consider collaboration as a principle, not just a tool

Collaboration is the key to helping your child survive and thrive with ADD. Collaboration, as I define it here, involves parents taking on the roles of coach and cheerleader. More importantly, collaboration involves your child's active participation. It involves your child thinking about exactly what is causing the attention and performance problem and what can be done to improve it.

The advantages of a collaborative model are numerous. They include helping your child to have greater awareness of ADD and its impact on their life. Collaboration also helps your child take greater ownership in the entire process of identifying, treating, and coping with ADD. Better results can be achieved when your child is a partner in the whole process. Collaboration should be seen as a principle not just a tool. It should inform every thought, every action and every decision from beginning to end. The more your child is able to cope and manage with his own effort, the more likely he or she will be able to function independently and successfully in the future.

Step 1: Select a time, setting and tone that will encourage dialogue

Let's assume you are at the beginning stage of exploring ADD issues. Don't rush this process. Bring the attention issues up at a time when there are no major conflicts erupting. You want to bring it up at a time when there can be some thoughtful consideration, some active listening, and some considered reflection. You want to bring it up at a time when your child is not frustrated and anxious, or exhausted and tired. This topic can't be crammed into the 15-minute drive to soccer practice.

Pick the right setting. Try to select a quiet place away from distraction and interruption. If you can't find it at home, consider selecting a "do not disturb" zone in a room with a door. Post a sign if necessary. If possible, it should not be in your child's room; there may be too many distractions.

The tone needs to be one of curiosity not criticism. You and your child together need to become detectives, looking for clues to solve the mystery of the attention problem and what can be done about it. Use the term "detectives;" it is less threatening and provocative. Sometimes the causes can be simple and obvious; for example, the homework didn't get done because your child wanted to play a game. Most often there are reasons that lie underneath the obvious. Yes, the game may have been an attractive alternative, but a deeper reason may be that your child can't stay focused on tasks or your child may have skill problems in reading, writing, or math.

Step 2: Show empathy

Introduce empathy as soon as possible. Empathy is your ally. Empathy is more than saying, "I'm sorry you have ADD." Empathy is conveyed when you describe your child's likely experience. For example, you might state, "I know you feel you can never finish," or "It is probably really hard to wait," or "You must feel buried in work that can't be done." Share examples of your own ADD-like experience where you avoided a task as a child, or even recently as an adult. Share an example when you got angry over some change of plans or some surprise work added to your schedule. Discuss your surface reasons, e.g., "I didn't like that job," then discuss the real, underlying reasons that contributed to your avoidance, e.g., "I really didn't think I could do it well." Your job here is to model self-examination strategies.

Ask your child if they have any ideas about how you could improve your own focus on tasks. You are modeling help-seeking behavior here. By helping another, you learn yourself. It also promotes collaboration and reduces defensiveness. Remember, you are modeling self-examination for your child. Your child might actually have some good advice for you! Maybe you have ADD too! Thank your child for their effort and suggestions. You are modeling how they can learn to accept observations and suggestions.

Step 3: Minimize short term expectations and maximize long term expectations

Parents typically open up a discussion with the expectation that a problem will be solved right away. They often expect the child to be able to analyze things quickly, own their deficiencies, apologize for their actions and finally fix it. That's not going to happen. Open up your discussion about ADD with the stated expectation that this is just the first step and that it will take several discussions to figure out how they might perform better and avoid problems at home or at school. Be sure to talk in specifics as much as possible. Cite specific attention-related problems that are concerning to you or their teachers and avoid broad negative labels such as "you are lazy" or "you are impatient."

Remind your child that you are both learning about ADD and you will get better at managing it over time. Keep a positive long-term outlook even if the short-term outlook looks pretty bleak. Most ADD children actually do survive and function well in spite of the ADD. They learn to adapt and cope. Tell them that. We want them to thrive, not just survive.

In that positive light, I can offer some thoughts from a 10-year-old patient of mine many years ago. When asked if he thought he had ADD, he agreed he did have ADD. He went on to comment, "I feel sorry for people without ADD." When asked why he felt that way, he responded, "People without ADD have a boring life. They don't see things like I do. They don't like to discover things. They don't have as much fun." He is correct. ADD does not have to be a burden pushing children and adults to frustration and failure. Correctly identified and managed, ADD can be an asset.

Reader Question: I am surprised at this child's attitude. I imagine most parents and teachers must convey a negative view of ADD and therefore a negative opinion of the child. Did this young man have special parents and counseling to come to this positive view?

Yes, the parents were certainly supportive. However, like all parents, they had their moments when they were frustrated with him. This positive attitude on the part of parents starts with an enlightened understanding of ADD. Parents need to not take ADD as a personal matter. Your child is not trying to drive you crazy or take control of the family. You and your child need to see light at the end of the tunnel. Finally, bringing the child into the self-management role, with parents acting as a coach, also helps all parties see this as a workable problem with a positive long-term outcome.

Step 4: Define the attention problem

When you suggest to your child that certain problems at home or at school might be caused by an attention problem, be more specific. Consider that attention problems can occur all along the information processing highway. Maybe your child is thinking of something else when you or the teacher is speaking. Maybe they drift off in their thinking after a few sentences. Maybe they misunderstood what was asked of them. Maybe on the way to do a task, they got distracted and did something else instead. Maybe they got tired or felt overwhelmed and couldn't stay on track. Notice that you framed the attention problem in at least four ways: problems with the initial listening, problems with drifting during the processing or downloading, problems with executing the behavior due to distraction and problems with fatigue. State that the attention problem can be at the beginning, the middle or at the end – or in all of these areas.

By defining how attention problems can occur at many points and for different reasons, you are helping your child consider and accept the possibility of having ADD, rather than simply dismissing it because it doesn't fit their definition of ADD.

Remind them too, that attention problems don't only occur with external distractions. They can occur when they are trying to solve a problem in their head or find some information filed away in their head. They may almost get there, but then lose the thought. Again, empathize if possible. It's frustrating to have the answer "on the tip of your tongue."

Step 5: Define coaching and collaboration

You are probably more used to being an authoritarian parent figure. You probably see your role as largely to inspect and direct, rather than to coach. Taking a more directive approach may work often, but it tends to limit growth and it often promotes your child's opposition and avoidance. A coaching role on the part of the parent encourages the child to explore their own skills, solve problems, and build on new skills. Tell your child you prefer a coaching role rather than a probation officer role.

Ask your child what they think is the role of a coach. Tell them what your understanding is regarding the coaching role. The coach's role is to closely observe the players and to offer suggestions for improving the players' skills. A good coach listens well to his players and you will endeavor to do that. A good coach will also ask his players to contribute their own thoughts and ideas, and will encourage his players to try something that might help improve their game. As a parent, as well as their coach, you will make any final decisions about managing ADD. You would also expect them to later evaluate this plan and together you can modify whatever plan is in place. Nothing is set in stone. Everything can be changed as you go along.

Your child needs to begin to understand that you expect and encourage their participation in the process of learning to manage attention problems. Explain that collaboration means that you will be asking them to give you details about what is difficult for them, to share their frustrations, to suggest what others can do to help and to think about ways they might change and improve the situation at home and at school.

Assure them that your job as coach is to listen to them regardless of whether or not you agree with them. You may ask them to clarify or explain things so that you understand. You may need to think about what was said before you respond. This process will provide good modeling for your child to learn how to communicate about difficult matters.

Step 6: Ask what works already for them

You may be surprised to know that children actually do have ways to manage their ADD. They live with it daily. They have learned appropriate and not so appropriate coping strategies to manage their ADD. I am often surprised at how children do manage ADD on their own.

Ask your child, "What tricks do you use to help you pay attention?" If they are a bit reluctant, remind them that some of the tricks they use, they might not have even noticed. Point out what behavior you observed that may be a kind of coping strategy. For example, you might state, "I notice you close your eyes when you listen," or "I see that you like to rock a bit when you are thinking." Speculate that such behavior might help them focus better. They may do it naturally without thinking. Share an example of your own if you can, such as, "I sometimes have to walk around a bit to think better." It helps me to "wake up my brain."

After reflecting on this, they may offer other observations. They might say they try to write fast to not forget things. They might speak fast and interrupt to not forget things. They might scribble to hide spelling mistakes. They might go to the bathroom to be able to get up and move about. These coping strategies remind you and your child that they do have coping skills, and they do have the capacity to learn additional coping skills.

By identifying existing coping strategies, both appropriate and inappropriate strategies, you open up the idea that they can actually find ways to manage their attention. Furthermore, you expect them to do so. This encourages your child to take ownership in the problem and to take responsibility for change.

Step 7: Avoid being adversarial

It is tempting to fall back into lecturing and reprimanding. If you find you lost the "curious detective" tone discussed above, take a break. Your child may either ignore your tirades, withdraw, shut down, or they will argue and counter attack. If you feel you are walking down this dead end road, turn back. Stop yourself and announce out loud, "I think I'm yelling and repeating myself. I need a few minutes timeout to stop, cool off and think about this some more. Probably you do too." Arrange a time to meet again an hour or two later. Of course, short term sanctions (e.g., no electronics) remain in place until answers are found and a plan to fix the problem is ready.

Step 8: Avoid being over controlling

Parents often decide they need to manage every aspect of their child's life in order to avoid catastrophe. This may seem to extend from the break of dawn until bedtime. Parents often orchestrate and direct such things as clothes being laid out, nagging constantly about getting teeth brushed, pushing to get the bed made, checking back packs, etc. The parent can be seen within several feet of the child's orbit, observing every movement like a surveillance satellite. This resumes after school with probation officer intensity. Parents check frequently on their child as a fifteen-minute homework assignment morphs into a three-hour battle of wills. Who is in charge here? Like the rat in the experimenter's maze, are we training the rat to run or is the rat training us to give him food? Is our child training us to expect less, to do part of the work or to just plain give up?

I have often seen ADD children who prefer to have their parents organize their work, lay out the materials needed, check every ten minutes, and correct mistakes too if needed. It is easier for them to be helpless and let others intervene. ADD children learn early on that the more they do, the more work they get. Conversely, the less they do, the less work they get. They probably don't consciously plan this strategy; it just works out that way.

In keeping with our collaboration theme, your child needs to assume more control over identifying, correcting and monitoring problems or tasks. Your job as coach is to have a dialogue with your child about how you can relinquish some of this control and how they can take over self-management duties. Start with small tasks. Have your child make small decisions first such as how to prepare for a friend's visit, where to put their toys, what time (within reason) will be devoted to homework or studying.

Reader Question: What if my child really is just trying to control us? What if he's not really just stressed out about how to do the work? What if it isn't a skills or an ADD issue? Maybe he just doesn't want to do homework, so he blows up to wear us down. There may not be any ADD problem here, just laziness.

That is possible. Your child may have learned to throw temper tantrums or cry a lot to get out of doing things at home or at school. But keep in mind that there is a big cost to a child who uses angry outbursts or crying meltdowns. Even if he or she "wins" with angry outbursts by avoiding some task, there is a punishment and rejection by others. Ask yourself, why would a child go such extremes to avoid simple tasks? Most kids don't go to these extremes. They negotiate or nag. Children without ADD may test limits, but eventually comply to avoid punishment and restrictions. Consider that temper may be a kind of coping strategy for children with attention or skill problems.

Ask yourself is there evidence of an ADD problem beyond the homework issue. If you see evidence of attention problems across many aspects of your child's life, even in their personal interactions with peers and family, it's likely to be true ADD. Discuss your observations about suspected attention problems beyond this current conflict. Ask for your child's thoughts and opinions.

Ask your child calmly and with a curious "detective" attitude why he or she has to go to such extremes to avoid doing a small task. Maybe he or she struggles with staying on the task, both in school and at home, resulting in avoidance of homework. However, there may be a skill problem here. Maybe your child struggles with writing, and therefore resists written homework. Maybe your child has reading problems, and therefore resists reading homework. Of course, your child may have both ADD and skill problems.

Dr. Leon Schofield

Step 9: Don't be deterred by "I don't know"

It's nothing personal. Children will almost always respond with "I don't know" at the first hint of a question. Even adults struggle with the "why" question. I bet you often don't know why you said or did something inappropriately or incorrectly. You often have to think about it for a while. With your child, don't settle for the simple, easy reasons; dig deeper.

Your child may know "why," but doesn't want to say it in order to avoid having to deal with a bigger problem. Your child may be "tired of homework," "I couldn't wait," or "I hate writing." All of these "excuses" offer some valuable hints. Remember, just listen, inquire, clarify and learn. Gradually your child will reveal the true difficulties focusing, listening, processing, remembering, writing, etc. Have empathy, if possible. If that's not possible, anticipate empathy: "I would like to understand your attitudes and feelings but it's still difficult right now. Let me ask more questions so I can understand."

Reader Question: OK, I am beginning to see your slant on ADD. However, I wonder about severity issues. Aren't some ADD children easer to help than others? Isn't there a continuum from mild to severe?

Yes, there certainly is a wide range of severity when we look at ADD. However, I want to caution parents on this matter. There are many ADD children who look quite severe and who may have many emotional and behavioral issues that complicate treatment. Many of these children can be treated very well with and without medication, with the right targeted interventions. They are not hopeless. Conversely, some ADD children may appear to be "mild" if they don't demonstrate obvious behavioral problems. However, they may be actually pretty severe on the ADD spectrum. Try not to prejudge. They may sit quietly without disturbing others, but still be very inattentive.

Get good data, good support at school, and good treatment. Don't try to judge severity by obvious symptoms. After you have collected real data, and after you have collected opinions of teachers and other professionals, you should be more able to identify where your child is on the ADD continuum.

Age appropriate collaboration

At this early stage of discussing the nature of ADD and how it may affect your child, there is little to collaborate on except possibly identifying the problems you see at home or the teacher sees at school. Your initial discussions should include your expectations regarding their participation in the entire process of investigating and fixing any attention problems. Your child should try to identify the frequency of problems, the setting, time of day and the nature of the tasks. Look for patterns. Detective work can narrow the problem down to some workable target.

If your child is skeptical or unsure about this process, acknowledge the lack of enthusiasm. Let them know that you too are trying out this new approach. Let them know you are doing some reading about this sort of thing in the hopes of learning some new tips on performing better. You are modeling future coping strategies; i.e., learning to do better by reading, learning and practicing new approaches.

Younger children might be asked to think about how they learned to ride a bike or tie their shoes. They had to watch, ask questions, practice, etc., in order to learn. The same is true regarding improving their ability to pay attention. Younger children might be able to dictate a list of examples of bad attention and the trouble it may cause children or adults. Older children may read portions of this book you have selected. They might go on line to look at definitions of

ADD. They might keep a journal of attention successes and failures during their day.

Question: Collaboration is important because:

    a. It allows my child to feel some ownership in the process.

    b. It starts right away to put some responsibility for change on my child.

    c. It reduces power struggles at home and at school.

    d. It helps my child become more proactive and independent.

    e. It reduces the fatigue and frustration of parents by having your child do much of the work.

    f. All of the above

Chapter 2: Consider Objective Testing to Diagnose ADD

ADD is a complex problem

Getting a good diagnosis is not as simple as it sounds. There are two main types of ADD: the hyperactive-impulsive type (ADHD) and the inattentive type. They each have different symptoms, different underlying causes and different ways to treat them. When assessing ADD, it is important to determine the severity of the ADD as well as the type. Many ADD children can cope well with milder types of ADD, with only minor accommodations. Others may need a wider range of accommodations and support, as well as a wider range of treatment.

In this chapter the pros and cons of using the medically accepted symptom lists and the pros and cons of using rating scales will be discussed. Family history of ADD will also be discussed as part of the evaluation process. The rationale for further objective testing will be reviewed. Testing data is quite valid and reliable. It definitely helps guide the educational planning process far better than report cards and rating scales. Strategies for obtaining such testing will be discussed. Suggestions will be offered to help your child collaborate in this process.

Step 1: Use official ADD symptom lists as an initial rating scale

The American Medical Association's Diagnostic and Statistical Manual V (DSM-5) © lists nine common characteristics of both types of ADD. While technically not a rating scale, these symptoms are commonly accepted symptoms of ADD and they should be considered in the earliest stages of your investigating possible ADD. If you have six of the nine characteristics of **hyperactive** impulsive ADD you likely have it.

- fidgety, restless
- difficulty remaining seated
- excessive physical activity or restless feelings
- difficulty playing or working quietly
- feeling "driven," can't stop
- talking excessively
- blurting out answers or comments
- difficulty waiting
- interrupting or intruding in conversations or activities

If you have six out of nine of the symptoms below you are likely to have **inattentive** type ADD.

- poor attention to details, careless mistakes
- difficulty with sustained attention
- poor listening when spoken to directly
- difficulty with instructions
- poor organization
- avoiding, procrastinating
- easily distracted
- forgetful in daily activities

According to the AMA there is also a third type of ADD. It is called the "**combined type,**" where the child has significant characteristics of both inattentive ADD and hyperactive-impulsive ADD. In my experience it is fairly rare to find this type of ADD. Usually if you look closely, the balance is tipped either to hyperactive or inattentive ADD.

Since it is often difficult to say a clear cut "yes or no" when considering these symptoms, I ask parents or child rate each symptom as "yes, no, or half and half." The use of a "half and half" option helps to avoid the risk of over or under rating the ADD. It allows for registering problem areas when they may occur fairly often but with varying activities, time of day, motivation, etc.

Rating scales, the pros and cons

There are several ADD rating scales such as the Conner's ADD scales© that are commonly used by pediatricians and school staff. All rating scales generally ask teachers and parents to rate their child on many symptoms or characteristics, indicated the frequency or severity on a broad scale, e.g., none or mild to frequent or severe. Your child can also independently rate himself in this early stage of investigating the ADD. Often the ratings are quite similar.

If parent and child ratings vary greatly, there may be some difference in interpreting terms. Make sure your child understands the terms, such as "restless." There also can be simple denial. In these cases it is a good idea to investigate possible reasons for your child's resistance to the whole idea of ADD. Perhaps your child is worried about having to change classes, get tutoring, take medication, etc.

The chief problem with rating general symptoms of ADD or rating numerous characteristics of ADD with lengthy questioning is that ratings are subjective. The ratings given may vary with the setting or the demands of the task. For example, one parent may rate their child higher since they supervise homework and chores. The other parent may have lower ADD ratings since they may see their child more at play or during outside activities.

The ratings may vary depending on the time of day. For example, a child may be more focused initially, but he or she may lose focus as the school day wears on. The ratings may vary with the personality of the rater; i.e., their level of tolerance of the ADD symptoms. For example, one teacher may see the child as disruptive and overly talkative while another teacher may see the child as enthusiastic and "loves to participate." The ratings may vary also due to the child's interest and motivation for the task. For example, you may see less of an attention problem with activities such as labs or drawing, but much greater attention problems when writing long passages.

The type of ADD the child has can also affect the rating scale results. In my opinion, hyperactive-impulsive ADD children tend to be rated higher for ADD, since they are more obvious and disruptive. Yet they may process and hear more than we think. On the other hand, inattentive ADD children tend to be underrated because the child is likely to be quiet and passive. They actually may process far less than they appear to be processing.

Though flawed, there are some pros to rating scales. Rating scales open the conversation about ADD. They help suggest the many ways attention problems can manifest itself. It can help to see the many faces of ADD and to not just consider ADD as only obvious out of control behavior. The rating scales can often say more about the frustration and concern of the rater more than an actual objective measure of the severity of the ADD. Rating scales are quick, easy to administer and inexpensive. They also can administered and scored by almost anyone, not just by trained psychologists.

I have no objection to completing rating scales as a starting point. However, in my opinion, they should not be used primarily or exclusively to determine the diagnosis.

Step 2: Strongly consider objective psychological testing

Even though objective testing can be expensive and time consuming, you should consider going beyond the rating scales if you feel that the diagnosis of ADD is marginal; i.e., still somewhat unclear based on rating scales numbers. You should consider objective testing if you want to have objective evidence for academic and treatment interventions. You should consider objective testing if want baseline data to measure improvements later after medication or educational accommodations have been in place for a while. You should consider objective testing data to help you to advocate for remedial services in school. With older children, objective testing data completed within three years is required by all standardized testing services (SAT, ACT), and virtually all colleges, including community colleges, if you are seeking extended testing time or other accommodations.

Parents may ask the school to provide objective testing. Many schools provide a fairly extensive package of testing options to measure basic ability to process incoming information. I would strongly recommend the Woodcock Johnson Tests of Cognitive Abilities©, which measure such important factors as:

- cognitive efficiency, or the ability to quickly and accurately process new information and retrieve stored information
- processing speed, or the ability to quickly scan visual information
- working memory, or the ability to hold several thoughts while downloading new information
- auditory processing, or the ability to hear and understand subtle differences in sounds
- short term auditory and visual memory, or the ability to quickly download and hold briefly, new information that can be stored later
- higher level reasoning, or the ability to problem solve, following several steps or operations without getting lost or sidetracked

Schools also offer achievement testing which helps determine academic skill levels compared to their peers. Schools should be able to provide thorough testing of basic academic skills in reading, writing and math. I find many ADD children actually have good skills, but they just don't use them in everyday work due to the ADD. However, I also often find many ADD children have at least moderate skill deficits in addition to the ADD, which may have been caused by years of inattention in class. I am more concerned about a child's future when I see poor skills as well as poor attention. Children with both attention and poor academic skills usually will need a more extensive array of remedial and support services, not just extended testing time in a quiet area.

Reader Question: OK, if I can convince the school to do extensive testing, that would be great. What if they refuse to do testing? What if they think your child is doing well enough for now and they just want to "wait and see" how things go before starting a battery of tests? What if they only give partial or limited testing and I don't feel it is sufficient?

If you disagree with a school's findings, most states allow parents to seek a second opinion; i.e., additional testing privately at the school's expense. Of course, the school administrators may be not too excited about this. They prefer to test "within house." Still, if you are not satisfied with the testing done at school, check the education laws in your state. You can look that up online or you can ask the school administrators directly. You may be entitled to a second opinion at the school's expense. Only do so if you feel there are real problems with the type of testing given or not given, or problems with the interpretation of findings.

You can get a second opinion by researching and looking for a psychologist in private practice, experienced in ADD and educational testing. Look for a state licensed psychologist with considerable experience in ADD and learning disabilities testing. You can ask school administrators and school staff for a referral. They are likely knowledgeable about this since they read the reports of these psychologists regularly. Check too with your child's pediatrician. Your state's psychological association may also have a list of psychologists in your area with an ADD or learning disability expertise.

Reader Question: You have talked about the importance of collaboration. If rating scales are completed by parents and teachers, should the child be told about this? It is the parents and teachers that are completing these rating scales, not the child.

I like the fact that you are asking this question. You should always reflect on collaboration issues, no matter what you are doing, including the ratings. Your child is probably well aware that there are problems in his functioning. I see every reason to bring your child into the conversation. They should be aware that you and your child's teacher have concerns about their attention issues. Have your child consider how they would rate themselves on the list of symptoms. The lengthy rating scales may be a bit too much to handle, especially for younger children. You might select a dozen key questions and have your child rate themselves independently. Talk about your rating and discuss any differences that may have occurred in ratings by your child, yourself and the teacher. Ask your child why they think there are differences in how they rate themselves versus how teachers or you may rate them.

Reader Question: What if your child is older and he or she complains about poor focusing in high school or even early in their college years, with no prior history of testing or treatment for ADD? Can this be an ADD problem?

Testing can be done at any time based on performance problems. I often see young adults who have tried a few colleges with minimal success. Bright students can evade detection in their earlier school years with extra effort, but they find there is no place to hide in the demanding world of college. I have had the local university medical school refer some advanced medical students for ADD testing. In spite of their excellent test taking skills and perfect grades, they have trouble with daily demands and detailed paperwork in a busy medical center.

ADD for older adolescents and young adults does not have to be disabling; however, it can be a "quality of life issue." Marginal grades, marginal work performance, and reduced ability to manage daily demands can be both annoying and limiting in terms of daily functioning and in terms of setting longer term goals. My goal is to help children and adults reach their full potential, not half. My goal is to have young adults be able to choose one of several paths in life, and not be forced into narrow and limited choices.

Step 3: Examine genetics in your ADD assessment

Another consideration in the early stages of assessing ADD is genetics. Is there any evidence of ADD in the immediate family? Among cousins and uncles? Grandparents? Look carefully at the family tree. There may be ADD in the immediate family. Ask yourself, using the symptoms list, how would I have rated myself as a child? How about now as an adult? The physical hyperactivity may have diminished a bit over the years, which is typical for many hyperactive

ADD adults. But ADD adults may still have many of the other ADD symptoms.

A child's risk factor for ADD is much greater with a family history of ADD. However, family history-taking can be tricky. If I ask parents if there is ADD in the family, I often get a response of "no." A parent may not see their own ADD issues if they have completed school and if they have a job. However, they may still have functioned well below their potential academically and vocationally. Among parents and other extended family there may be limited education, frequent job changes, legal problems, alcohol or drug abuse, mental health problems, etc. These factors may mask an underlying ADD.

Step 4: Consider ADD testing if your child has emotional and behavioral problems

Some children may be labelled as having an oppositional-defiant disorder or a conduct disorder. Others may be labelled as having an anxiety disorder. ADD problems are often the cause of many of these emotional or behavioral problems. However, the emotional or behavioral problems may be severe, calling for immediate intervention and/or treatment. The ADD issues that may be ignored due to the various crises these children present. Be sure to investigate ADD issues even if they seem minor because they are dwarfed by the various crises in their day to day life.

You may find that intensive treatment of the emotional and behavioral problems will have only partial success. In these cases there may be undetected attention problems that promote the emotional and behavioral problems. It is also possible that your child may have two separate problems – ADD and anxiety. Treat them both.

Step 5: Consider ADD testing if your child has slipped in performance in later grades

Older children heavily involved in athletics can also avoid an ADD diagnosis because they have channeled much of their energy into sports. There is some evidence that daily aerobic exercise has some limited attention benefits for hyperactive ADD children. These sports-oriented children have been forced into being more efficient in their time management, in order to meet team commitments for training and sporting events. A more efficient work ethic can help manage ADD; however, in most cases grades for these students will suffer as the bar is steadily raised in the high school years.

Inattentive ADD children tend to slide below the radar for years since they are less annoying and less disruptive. They get into academic trouble in middle school and high school with a shift from learning by work sheets in elementary school to learning by lecture in middle school and high school. Also, there is much less teacher supervision in later grades and more work. Children in middle school and high school also have to move from class to class with various books and materials. Organization of their backpacks and lockers is often a challenge.

Many bright ADD children can do fairly well even through high school. In many of these cases, the child who is extremely bright may be good at quick scanning for important information and good at test-taking skills. In many cases there is also a "helicopter mom" in the background checking work, keeping their ADD child on track, etc. These children may not struggle until young adult years. These successful teens may be less successful in a college setting when the supervision and support of home and school are gone.

The old idea that ADD must be diagnosed in early childhood – e.g., by age seven – is incorrect. If your child is struggling with performing in later grades, there may be inattentive ADD issues. Objective testing can highlight these areas of weakness where rating scales and observational studies of your child may under estimate the severity of your child's difficulty in processing new information.

Step 6: If you are undecided about objective testing, re-examine this option later

You may choose to take a "wait and see" approach if your child's performance is adequate. You might be having some success in improving attention and performance with some behavior approaches or some minor accommodations at school or at home. Perhaps you may be trying tutoring after school. Maybe you are more closely supervising and monitoring the homework. If you have ADD concerns you should set a specific timetable to re-examine the need for testing. Perhaps six months out would be a good time to reconsider the need for testing. The tipping points for pursuing more in-depth testing involve several factors:

a. significant deficits continue in school performance
b. frustration and negative attitudes about school are continuing or increasing
c. self-esteem is low and worsening
d. resistance to school work continues
e. resistance to attending school continues
f. emotional problems such as anxiety, depression, sleep issues begin or worsen

If you feel your child has one or more of these red flags, in spite of reasonable efforts on your part and on the part of your child, you should strongly reconsider pursuing thorough testing.

Reader Question: Isn't testing done in a supervised setting with one adult watching you, in a small room with no distractions? How is that an objective measure of ADD? Wouldn't an ADD child do well in that setting?

I understand you may be reluctant to pursue testing for that reason. I agree that the testing room and the testing itself are artificial and may not reflect performance deficits found in a more distracting class environment. Don't forget, we are comparing the ADD child with peers of the same exact age without ADD, tested under these similar conditions. Deficiencies in attention will be shown as we compare with peers. If testing shows minimal or no attention deficits, then it suggests that modest modifications and accommodations in the classroom may work well. However, if testing shows significant attention deficits across a wide range of attention measures compared with his or her expected level of performance and compared with the typical performance of peers at their grade level, some accommodations will likely be needed. These accommodations will be described in the next chapter.

Age appropriate collaboration

You will need to be very specific about the symptoms of ADD before your child can judge or rate themselves. Younger children are not developmentally able to take on the perspective of others very well. They are rather self-centered, concrete and immediate in their focus. They don't understand abstract concepts very well, e.g., the term "restless." They don't have much of a future perspective and aren't able to consider what will happen next month or next year. You can and should use the standard words describing ADD but you should also give specific examples of those terms before asking a child to rate themselves. For example, you might ask about "restless." If they don't define that clearly and well, you can tell your child that means rocking or tapping at your desk. Consider too, how the symptom might differ with activity, setting and time of day. They may be more restless doing written work, for example. Or they may be more restless as the school day wears on.

In terms of testing, younger children usually accept this well. They can be told a school psychologist will see them in their office and ask them to answer some questions, do some puzzles and copy or write some things. Explain that this will be done on a few different occasions to determine what they do well and what they may struggle with. Explain as well that after it is done the results will be discussed with you and your child. You may have a private session with the school psychologist to review the results, but I would recommend a second session for your child with you as observer. Your child should ask questions and offer comments as the psychologist explains the results in simple, direct terms.

Older children are generally familiar with psychologists and testing at school. They probably have a few friends who have had testing and accommodations. Many ADD children tend to "flock together." However, they may still have more specific questions about what tests will be given. They may be concerned about what classes they might miss during testing. They may have concerns about possible changes down the road in their schedule, their class assignments or even changes in their school. Try to listen well, clarify and commit to getting answers.

If possible try to accommodate testing time to your child's needs. For example, with older students, I find that they are often concerned about missing required team practices or meets. They might prefer early morning testing and make up class work later. As far as the longer range implications, you can't make any guarantees about future educational planning. Commit to considering all options together with your child.

Question: Rating scales

a. Are a common means of diagnosing ADD
b. Are subjective and may vary by setting, task, rater's tolerance for ADD symptoms, etc.
c. Are quick, easy and cheap to administer
d. Are limited in what they reveal compared with cognitive abilities and achievement testing
e. Do not provide a comprehensive examination of your child's strengths and weaknesses
f. All of the above

Chapter 3: Seek Help from School Early

Getting help is a complicated process

We have already looked at how you can pursue ratings and testing to help determine the type and severity of your child's ADD. In this chapter the types of accommodations and services you may need for your child will be considered. Beyond ADD testing, you may also need input of specialists such as reading teachers, school psychologists, speech-language, and occupational therapists. After all relevant information is gathered, you will need to work with the school to develop an educational plan that will include specific accommodations and specific remedial services.

If your child is in a private school, they may not offer special services or accommodations. That shouldn't stop you from asking. As a taxpayer in your school district, you are likely to be entitled to testing services and remedial services from your local public school even if your child is enrolled in a private school or if your child is homeschooled. Special services such as speech-language therapy or occupational therapy may be provided to your child. You may have to arrange for transportation of your child to the public school for such services depending on the school district and state rules.

Typical accommodations for your child

Early intervention is important. The earlier that problems are identified and managed, the better the outcome. Don't be deterred by comments by others such as, "he's young; he'll grow out of it." While there is a wide range of development, and sometimes children do blossom a bit later than others, don't count on it. Trust your own instincts. Also, though your child's teachers may not push for testing or services, they often will send notes home suggesting that there may be a problem. Teachers may want to not offend parents by pointing out flaws in their children. Teachers may not want to overburden the school's resources. If your child's teacher subtly hints at the need for further evaluation, jump on it.

The most frequent help offered by schools is a 504 plan. This is a reference to Federal Law 504, which guarantees help for all children with any handicapping problem that interferes with learning, including ADD. Children can be given appropriate accommodations to help them perform at their ability level in a normal mainstreamed class environment. It is designed to level the playing field by providing modest accommodations to the educational plan. Usually this 504 plan involves:

- Extended testing time in a quiet area
- Checks on understanding of oral or written directions
- Preferential seating up front
- Allowing some movement, standing at times, breaks
- Special chair cushion, to allow movement without distracting others

Older children often need:

- Copy of teacher's notes
- Laptop or tablet for writing
- Use of calculator for math tests
- Use of tape recorder or digital pen for note taking
- Breaks during testing

Some children need even more assistance and accommodations. These additional accommodations usually fall under an IEP (Individual Education Plan). These accommodations can require changes in teaching methods, testing methods, and even in changes in educational requirements. The additional accommodations might include:

- Reduced homework workload
- Elimination of some required courses
- Smaller classroom setting, with an additional teacher aide
- Special study hall to explain and supervise assignments and projects
- Dictation of answers for homework and tests
- Special services such as (occupational therapy, physical therapy, speech and language therapy, and counseling)
- Remedial services in reading, writing, math

The line between a 504 plan and an IEP is a blurry one. What degree of ADD is needed for either a 504 or an IEP varies a bit across school districts. Some 504 plans have more significant accommodations typical of an IEP while some IEPs can look rather minimal, much like a 504 plan.

Step 1: Prepare for a 504 or IEP

Start the process with a couple of meetings with your child's teacher or teachers. Get work samples. Ask if your child's teacher about your child's:

- Academic skills deficiencies in reading, writing or math
- Initial ability to focus and listen accurately
- Quickly drifting off-task
- Tiring, with increasingly sloppy or careless work
- Ability to sit quietly
- Tendency to frustrate easily and quit
- Disruptiveness in class

If you and your child's teacher see problems, it's time to look into a 504 plan. The 504 plan can be started by a simple written request to the principal indicating you would like to address your child's educational needs at a meeting for the purpose of starting a 504 plan. Be short, clear and concise. Specifically cite examples of deficient skills and weak performance on homework, desk work, and tests as well as your observations and teacher observations. Attach to your written request an addendum with a sample of work, if possible. A picture is worth a thousand words. You may sell your point right away by showing a copy of a clearly messy, disorganized homework paper your child should have been able to quickly complete. Request that the principal get back to you in a reasonable time, e.g., a week. Try to schedule a 504 meeting as soon as possible. Be polite and thankful for their anticipated help.

A 504 meeting will include the principal, teacher(s), school psychologist and possibly another teacher relevant to your child's needs (physical education, art or music). It will likely be in a small conference room or in the principal's office. You will usually be invited to bring along someone who knows or works with your child, e.g., counselor, private psychologist, tutor, special education advocate, another parent. Feel free to bring along such people to weigh in or to be another listener to make sure you didn't miss anything.

If, after you hear the proposed plan, you feel more significant changes need to be in your child's educational plan, you can request an individual educational plan (IEP). Your written request for an IEP goes through a special committee called the CSE, Committee for Special Education. They meet regularly to evaluate and prioritize requests before setting up a meeting. In most school districts you are entitled to a CSE meeting and that must be set up reasonably quickly, usually in thirty business days.

A formal CSE (Committee for Special Education) meeting usually includes a broader mix of school staff. In addition to those attending a 504 meeting, the participants often include a few specialists, such as speech-language teacher, occupational therapist, reading specialist, school nurse and a parent advocate. It usually also includes a secretary to take minutes of the meeting. This type of meeting is more formal and includes more professional staff since it addresses changes that may be needed in the actual educational requirements. For older children, several teachers may be involved.

As with a 504 plan, I encourage parents to have a few meetings with key players who work with your child before the IEP meeting occurs to collect data and record concerns, as well as to give these teachers and specialists a "heads up" so they can be prepared to advocate for your child. A date will be offered and you will be notified in writing. You will be advised as well that you can bring along any advocate or professional you wish, including an attorney specializing in education law.

Reader Question: Wait a second. Won't bringing an attorney along create unnecessary problems? I want to have a cooperative, working relationship with the school, not an adversarial one.

If you approach this in a polite and candid manner, there will not be any problem. For example you might state, "I will be bringing along an attorney familiar with educational law. I really don't know much about this area." Most school districts will remind you that you have a right to bring an attorney to a 504 or IEP meeting. School staff are more likely to follow procedures and not try to push their recommendations. Also, you can indicate in advance that you will want to review any proposed plans with your attorney after the meeting before agreeing to any changes in the educational plan.

At the conclusion of the either a 504 or IEP meeting the chairperson will generally propose some changes in your child's educational plan. The chairperson usually will ask you to sign a form stating that you agree to this new plan. You may find that satisfactory. However, you may want to think about it, discuss it with your child, consult with your child's psychologist, and review it with your child's pediatrician before signing off on the plan. If so, you can thank the committee for their input, but you will have to postpone signing any documents pending further review.

If you disagree with the proposed plan or if school staff feel there is no need for a 504 or IEP plan, I advise parents to consider two paths. First, you may want your objections or concerns recorded for the record. You then might want to set a short-term goal; i.e., a time frame of a few months to revisit the educational plan in place and then reconsider options. This sends the message that you are keeping a close watch, you aren't going away, you won't tolerate a wasted year and you are prepared to be an ongoing advocate for your child.

Second, you have a legal right to appeal any 504 or IEP decision in most states. Check the local and state education rules before you begin the process, or later if you have questions. You can always call the state education office and ask specific questions. In addition to private legal advice, there also may be independent, governmentally funded agencies in your area, such as the Advocacy for the Developmentally Disabled that can offer assistance and answer questions regarding your rights and options. These offices can provide free legal advice and even represent you at a future CSE meeting in some cases.

Step 2: Plan on having your child participate regularly in educational planning meetings

All children, at all ages should consider attending meetings at school related to their attention and/or academic problems. If a child is very anxious and has problems articulating their concerns, have your child dictate what is difficult for them in school and what they think would be helpful, in their own words. You can type it and print it. They can then sign it and that document can be distributed at the school meeting and it can be included in the child's record. Your child can then attend the meeting without comment. Or if your child is quite anxious, you can present your child's dictated document as you're their representative.

Reader Question: Is that really necessary? Won't it just be a waste of time and perhaps stressful for the child?

Remember the long range goal is to have a child become a self-sufficient adult. Part of that journey starts with learning to advocate for yourself, in small steps at first. Many children can attend such a meeting without any major stress and with minimal preparation. Mostly your child will be there to listen, and occasionally to offer an opinion about a specific accommodation that may be offered. You will mostly speak for them. Just being there signals to your child that they have rights and that they must learn to advocate for themselves over time.

Another side benefit of having your child at a 504 or IEP meeting is that it makes it more difficult for the committee to hurry the process or try to impose their will without at least listening. It tends to soften the group in my experience, especially if your child is able to speak about what distresses them and what might be helpful. The same can be said about distributing your child's work samples.

The sample vividly expresses the need better than volumes of your oral or written testimony.

Children can also suggest amendments to a proposed accommodation. For example, the child might need a quiet work area. It might be in the back of the class, it might be away from the window, it might be at the library. If they need help with writing, it might be possible to have an aide writing longer answers dictated by your child. The standard extended testing time accommodation might not be needed. Some children don't need extra time, they just need breaks every twenty minutes or so. Your child's input can be helpful in refining a proposed accommodation.

If the evaluation shows the need for support services, make sure those services are in place. Make sure that these services are included in the formal 504 or IEP documents. Your child may need extra help in reading, since ADD children are usually behind in this area. They may also need writing assistance. An OT (occupational therapist) can help. They might prescribe exercises for school and home settings for fine motor (writing) and gross motor (coordination) skills. Speech-language therapists can help with receptive and expressive language skills. They can help your child seek help appropriately, advocating for themselves by working on scripts that your child can practice. They can help with socializing issues. Counselors and school psychologists may help your child address self-esteem issues, anxiety and peer relationship concerns.

Reader Question: Is this kind of school management possible for busy parents? Shouldn't the school be the expert here? I don't know much about education. It sounds like it should be primarily the school's job to educate ADD children.

Pay me now or pay me later. The time you can devote to early intervention will save you and your child much in time, money and aggravation down the road. It may sound like a huge time commitment, but it is actually not that bad. Much of the preliminary work can be done by email or calls to your child's teachers and other staff. School meetings can be done very early in the morning or after school. They will be short and direct. There is no time to chitchat with the school buses on the way. The 504 and IEP meetings are usually an hour and generally are on time. Follow-up meetings can be email or brief early morning visits. You don't have to hover over teachers and staff, but you do have to keep them focused on your child with follow-up notes and visits.

Step 3: Monitor the accommodations in place

Educational plans are simply the best guess about how to help your child. Parents should be prepared to be vigilant throughout the school year. Parents should meet with teacher(s) at least quarterly to monitor progress and to adjust the plan a bit to improve things. If any major changes to the plan are needed, likely it will have to go back to the 504 committee or the full CSE committee meeting for approval. You don't want to wait until close to the end of the school year to make changes.

Ask your child often if they are being offered accommodations as described in the 504 plan or IEP plan. Just as importantly, ask if they are using those accommodations. If not, why not. Avoid being critical here. For example, parents often tell their child to ask for help if they don't understand something or if they need to have things repeated. That's all very good, but perhaps your child is trying to avoid criticism by the teacher or aid ("You should be listening better."), avoid having the teacher over-explain something ("Let's go over everything; pay attention.") when there is only a small detail that needs to be explained, or avoid having to spend extra time on an onerous task.

The accommodations may need to be adjusted to fit your child's needs, which may change during the course of the school year. Your child's teacher's approach to educating your child may need to be adjusted as the year progresses. Your child also needs to become more proactive and assertive. Don't forget to have some empathy here, including for your child's teacher.

Reader Question: When are all these accommodations "too much?" Maybe our child needs to have a small class or even homeschooling.

Generally the benefits of mainstreaming outweigh the costs. It is a delicate balance though. If your child is spending half of his day for pullout intervention services, that may be a problem. If your child dreads school and doesn't feel he is improving with all of these accommodations, that is a problem. Further tweaks in the services or in the educational plan may be needed. However, a smaller self-contained classroom setting with greater supervision and one-to-one services may be needed. Home schooling can be an option, but it is not an option for many parents.

Step: 4: Consider obtaining assistance outside of school

You may want to have private assistance outside of the school. The reasons for this are that most assistance in school will involve pulling out your child for special services. They may miss important work and there is a bit of stigma for some children. Special help outside of the classroom may also be rather brief – e.g., once or twice a week – and there may be three or more students involved. This could limit the true amount of time given for remedial work. Some 504 plans and IEPs will have "consulting" specialists who work with the teacher in class to have the teacher do the remedial work. Some such programs will have an aide in the classroom to float around and help a few students. This may reduce the "pullout problem," but the intervention and support is rather limited by the nature of the situation.

You may want to inquire about what services are available to you privately, to supplement school services or to continue services through vacations and summer. You can find outside help for your child with licensed professionals who provide services individually. You can also find private educational centers in most communities that will work on academic skills in small group settings.

You can also find outside tutors for specific subjects to help your child. Your school should have a list of approved private tutors in your area. One big advantage to a private tutor is that the material can be modified to meet the student's attention and skill levels, slowing the presentation and repeating things as needed. Another advantage is that the child is likely to accept help more readily from this person than from you. You don't want to be the "homework police" all the time. It's nice to give yourself a little break. You are then able to talk about less stressful subjects and even enjoy one another at times.

Step 5: Make sure retesting is done as required

Generally speaking, the school will retest children every three years. In the case of the more modest accommodations found in a 504 plan, this may be very minimal, perhaps only giving rating scales for teachers and parents. For an IEP, the retesting is typically more thorough and complete. I would ask about exactly what tests will be done. They should be at least as extensive as the earlier assessment for comparison purposes. Some schools may want to do just a part of a test or perhaps just rating scales by teachers and parents. That's not enough to make any intelligent decisions moving forward, in my opinion. As grades advance there are big increases in quality and quantity of work expected. You might want to look at more extensive achievement testing to be sure your child has sufficient reading, writing and math skills to do the required work. The attention problems may have lessened, but the skills may still be weak.

As a child ages out in late high school, schools may not be too cooperative to do a complete evaluation in the senior year, just to help with college accommodations. You can lobby for it, but usually they will offer only prior records and a note indicating your child has been receiving accommodations from a certain date, through high school. You can get copies of records and a copy of prior testing if needed, of course. If you want to obtain testing accommodations for standardized testing accommodations (SAT, ACT, MCAT, LSAT, etc.) you will usually need an update in test data; i.e., testing battery usually within three years. If you must, you can find a licensed psychologist in private practice for this type of testing in your community. Make sure he or she has extensive experience in this matter.

Reader Question: Isn't there a danger of all this help hurting the child in the long run? Maybe it will cause colleges to reject them if they know the grades all have "extra time" footnotes attached. The same may be true if my child has extra time for standardized tests. Doesn't it highlight deficiencies in my child?

You might find some negative reactions. I'm not saying it will never happen. With the high numbers of students with accommodations today, it is often seen as pretty routine. Also, to be frank, most schools look at the GPA and standardized testing scores and they apply some cutoff. If the child makes the cutoff, a more thorough screening of the record may pass through the hands of an application reviewer. Some parents address ADD and learning disabilities proactively in the essay portion by having their child write about the various accommodations and how that has been beneficial. If the accommodations were reduced or eliminated, note this as well.

The student should also request an interview at the school he or she would like to attend. Usually notes are taken by the interviewer and these are included in the application packet. Generally an in-person interview puts your application higher in the acceptance pile.

Step 6: Advocate for your child

Most schools are pretty tight on time and money. They have a lot of state mandated testing and retesting on their plate for students already receiving special educational interventions. Parents have to be the squeaky wheel. The school will tend to take a "wait and see" attitude. They will assume your child will mature and catch up. That is a gamble. If they are wrong, then you will have to deal with failure, significant deficits in academic skills, self-esteem issues, etc., along with the as yet untreated ADD. Parents need to be vigilant and persistent. You should:

- Always put your requests for services in writing, for the record.
- If testing is warranted, advocate for the most thorough testing available.
- Always keep copies of all correspondence.
- Write a thorough summary of phone conferences, dated.
- Keep a record of teacher notes, and samples of work.
- Meet at least quarterly with your child's teacher to assess attention as well as skills.
- Take notes with teachers' quotes.
- Always be thankful to your child's teacher; you need an advocate.

You should especially reinforce special efforts by teachers, psychologists and specialists who work with your child. They often have to make difficult decisions in the context of tight budgets and pressure to reduce services. They need our praise and support.

Don't toss your records after high school. You may need to locate old reports and school records for college, graduate school, professional schools (medical school, law school, etc.) and for state licensing exams in the future. Most schools and professionals will destroy old records after several years. State laws vary on record keeping. In New York, records must be kept for six years after a child's twenty-first birthday. Also, future doctors may be interested in old records if they are treating adult ADD. Your old records will be very useful.

Reader Question: Who should keep these records, a parent or our young adult ADD child? Shouldn't they be responsible for their own records?

That's a great question. I am a big advocate for teaching self-management. On the records point, I think it's not just an ADD problem. Recordkeeping is difficult for everyone, including adults without ADD. I would suggest having a serious discussion with your young adult ADD child about this. They may want to manage their old files and records, but they may prefer that you hold onto this data.

There may be practical reasons for your holding onto this information. Young adults are often moving. They have not yet fully developed their own information management system. They may still be struggling with organizational issues. If you are the guardian of the file, make sure they know where it is and how they can get it in case you are incapacitated later.

If they are going to manage the file, discuss a plan of action. Ask them to think about the reasons to secure this information. Ask them to consider where and how they would store this information. Ask them to make sure they communicate the manner and place of the storage to you or to their significant other as an additional safeguard.

Step 7: Avoid dependency

You can create a dependent child if you are not careful. Always remember that your ultimate goal is to have a self-sufficient adult who is capable of managing day-to-day demands. If you do too much you may send the message that they can't cope. They will always need to work at listening, clarifying, advocating for themselves. They will also need to work at organizing things, time management, and completing longer term tasks and projects. They will need to learn to appropriately ask for clarification, assistance and support. They will need to accurately judge their performance and correct problems. These factors can't be controlled by medication or extended testing time alone.

As your child gradually learns many of the coping skills discussed in this book, you can begin to withdraw some of your support. Even school accommodations may be unnecessary at some point. A trial period without such accommodations is often reasonable after the child has shown good performance. However, your child may always need extended testing time. Many children can self-manage rather well, but still struggle with tightly timed testing.

Reader Question: I have heard that getting either a 504 or an IEP is rather difficult. Why is that?

There are many reasons. In the early elementary years, there is a wide variation in skills and in children's rate of development, aggravated also by a pretty wide range of ages in the class. A child of five years and zero months of age is a very different child compared with a child of five years eleven months of age, though they may both be in the same kindergarten class. Still a "wait and see" approach is risky, since these days children are pushed hard and early to quickly develop basic core skills.

You certainly can wait and keep a close watch on your child's progress. Remember, I mentioned earlier that the child often will dictate the action needed by falling performance relative to peers, by increased negative emotions, behavior problems and by lowered self-esteem. These are all alarm bells for sure. There is the added risk that a child may slide by under the radar with low-average performance in early elementary grades. As that child hits late elementary school grades, there is far less opportunity for extra time in the school day to devote to academic skill-building. The extra time is used for subject matter. Pullout remedial services often compete with academic schedules in the later grades, just as the quality and volume of work demands increases exponentially. Investigate ADD early and act early.

Age appropriate collaboration

The involvement of your child in the educational planning is crucial. Without their participation, they will often resist or participate minimally. They need to have a stake in the game. There are several examples in many of the steps above regarding how you can bring your child into this process. Even younger children can participate in this educational planning. With some encouragement and support they can begin to identify problems they have in school and they can begin to offer potential solutions. Younger children may actually be easier to draw into this process. They enjoy having some control over how their lives will unfold at school.

Older children often prefer to be invisible. They want no extra attention. They want to blend in and fit in. They don't want to be seen as different. They can articulate their needs well, but they often choose not to do so. Older children need empathy for their dilemma, not criticism for their resistance to accept accommodations, remedial training or support services. They need to explore how such interventions can make a big difference in their success at school.

They need to consider more subtle interventions that support them without calling much attention. They need to work on being more proactive and they need to learn how to ignore potential joking or criticism of peers.

Older children need to see the longer term vision. They need to imagine the success that will follow college and further training, the freedom of having several options in their lives and the enjoyment they will have pursuing their interests. With a positive vision and a positive goal, the day-to-day frustrations become less unpleasant.

Question: Parents can generate an educational plan for their child by:

a. Seeking feedback and support of the teacher
b. Preparing a summary of their child's recent problems
c. Having your child dictate a note outlining their problems and their suggestions for change
d. Filing a written request for a 504 or IEP plan with supporting documents
e. Encouraging your child to attend 504 and IEP meetings at school
f. Monitoring the plan at least quarterly and changing the 504 or IEP if needed
g. All of the above

Dr. Leon Schofield

Chapter 4: Know the Limitations of Medication

Disclaimer

I am a Ph.D. licensed clinical psychologist. I am not a medical doctor and I am not licensed to write prescriptions. I can, however, describe how medications effect the brain and give my observations on how they affect my patients. I recommend that parents become educated in medication usage for ADD. There are many books and magazine articles out there for this purpose. Some parents like to participate in chat rooms on line to get firsthand advice. I would be cautious with some testimonials in this regard. Parents often have a very biased view on whether to medicate or not, or on what type of medication is best. Remember, each child is very different, and their medication experiences might not be the same for your child. Consult with your pediatrician regarding medication options.

A short history of medication management of ADD

Ever since we fell in love with science, we have come to believe that medications can fix almost anything, including ADD. Medication for ADD has been around for quite a while now, with some spectacular results and some less so.

In 1937 in the American Journal of Psychiatry, Dr. Charles Bradley published one of the earliest studies using amphetamine medications to treat inpatient adolescents with serious emotional and behavioral problems. He speculated that stimulant medications activated the frontal portion of the brain. That part of the brain is the basic manager for the brain. It helps us decide what to do and when to do it. It helps us stay focused and problem solve. Activating the frontal lobes of the brain with stimulant medication, he reasoned, would help with attention and overall behavior. He found that about half of the kids improved immediately in their school work with stimulant medication. They even improved emotionally. Unfortunately half of the children had agitation and anxiety issues and didn't improve at all. You can guess which of these kids had primarily hyperactive type ADD and which had mood disorders and thought disorders.

Further study was suggested, but not much research was done using stimulants for children until nearly twenty years later, when psychiatrists started again to treat hyperactive type ADD kids with stimulants. Similar findings of rapid improvement were noted. The use of stimulants continued to climb steadily through the 1980s. ADD was considered to be a childhood disorder until then and it was not treated beyond the teen years. Many psychologists began to wonder what happens later to these children placed on stimulants for eight to ten years or more. Studies showed that many ADD children, grown up, without continued treatment, did not do very well academically or vocationally. They also were more likely to have various emotional and behavioral problems.

Since the 1990s most psychologists and physicians have come around to the idea that ADD is life-long and needs to be managed in the adult years as well as in childhood. Some adults may learn to cope with it better than others, and they can manage fairly well without medication. Others struggle with academic, vocational and social functioning. It is likely that those with more severe ADD fall into this latter group.

To complicate the picture, in the early 1990s researchers began to diagnose inattentive type ADD. These children had little or none of the hyperactivity and impulsiveness of the children diagnosed in earlier years. The chief problem for these children is that they have struggles with processing or downloading new incoming information, written and oral. They also have problems drifting off-task. Inattentive ADD was quickly accepted as a genuine disorder and it was diagnosed in many children. Inattentive ADD children are in many ways the opposite of the hyperactive ADD children.

The inattentive ADD child is likely to process incoming information slowly and miss much of the oral and written material. They frequently drift off-task. However, since they are not disruptive, they often don't get diagnosed early. They often slide downward in performance by middle school where they face greater work, more lecture-based learning, and challenging schedules. There also is a kind of safety net in elementary school. Teachers know your child well, dealing with them all day. They may make unofficial accommodations without any formal 504 plan.

In addition to the expansion of the diagnostic system to include inattentive type ADD, there have been advances in medication. The chief change has been the development of longer acting stimulants, often for a full twelve hour effect. This stopped the noon trips to the nurse's office at school. Older children are often given a second dose of a short acting stimulant after school to help with homework, sports, family life, etc.

A child struggling with attention is headed for trouble. Your child deserves to have a positive and productive life with family and friends, not just at school. Medication may be needed to help your child function well. Here are some steps to consider if you are contemplating medication as a treatment option.

Step 1: Consult with your doctor

Pediatricians are the first line of defense. Parents most often bring their concerns to their child's doctor who usually makes a decision about medication after a history-taking and after parents and teachers complete a rating scale. This process was discussed in chapter 3. They usually will follow up with a brief interview with parent and child. Prescribing stimulants can vary. Some doctors use stimulants for school only, others daily. Some pediatricians may prefer to refer your child to a pediatric neurologist or a pediatric psychiatrist for evaluation and treatment of ADD. Your pediatrician might prefer that a specialist manages the medication.

Stimulants don't need a long time to reach full effectiveness, like many other medications. They work immediately and effectively, first day, first dose. You may not see much improvement at lower dosages, but the medication is truly working right away! Stimulants are up and working in about a half hour or so.

The common, expected side effects reported by children are decreased appetite mid-day and increased thirst. Stimulants are known appetite suppressants and also they tend to dehydrate. These common side effects are almost a good sign, to me, as they signal the medication is working. These expected side effects are rather minor and can be managed easily by eating small quantities more often and by drinking more water. Often these normal side effects lessen over time. Of course, the bad side effects are the stimulating symptoms which we would expect from amphetamines, such as agitation, temper, restlessness, stronger emotional reactions, headaches, sleep problems, etc. You should contact your pediatrician if these side effects occur. Adjustments in timing, dosage or type of stimulant may help. Your doctor will monitor medications regularly, monitoring blood pressure, heart rate, weight, etc.

You can try stimulants with either type of ADD. Based on my observations over the years, stimulants seem to have more dramatic and positive effect with less risk of side effects for hyperactive types of ADD, compared with inattentive ADD. However, I have seen modest gains with the inattentive ADD children too. Stimulants are short-lived medications, and generally get along well with other medications. But always check with your doctor. A family history of ADD, diagnosed or suspected, supports the use of medication, particularly if stimulant medication was or is still part of their treatment history. Other factors that would tip the balance towards medication trials would be severity of your child's functional problems in and out of school, as well as the degree of punishment and restrictions imposed in and out of school. If your child's life is miserable, it's time to consider medication.

Step 2: Assess the risks of medication

With healthy children, side effects with medication, particularly for hyperactive type ADD, are minimal. Watch for tics or involuntary muscle contractions, which can often occur in facial muscles. These little twitches are often subtle, but observable if you are attentive. You should report any such concerns to your doctor. Often a modest reduction in dosage is sufficient to eliminate such problems. Your doctor may also want to try a different stimulant medication. Many children (and adults) can better tolerate a different stimulant. The two types of stimulants are amphetamine medications (Dexedrine, Vyvanse, Adderall) and methylphenidate medications (Ritalin, Concerta, Metadate). Switching to another medication within the class can be helpful because the delivery of the medication may be a bit different, e.g., faster or slower. Switching to another type of stimulant may also be helpful since there are slight chemical differences, though all stimulants work in a similar fashion.

Weight is a big issue for children. Since stimulants tend to suppress appetite, they will need to eat small quantities often during the day to avoid weight loss. Thirst is common. The dehydration accompanying stimulants can cause constipation. More water intake is needed all year, not just in the summer or when exercising. Again these are common reactions, not really side effects. They usually can be managed well.

Step 3: Consider the psychological effects of medication

A subtle issue is the psychological effects of medication. There can be an over-reliance on medication to fix everything. Medication tends to make us feel that the ADD problem is a medical one, controlled only or primarily by the medication. The common parent refrain is, "Did you take your medication?" when their child misbehaves. Children need to expect that medication will help, hopefully, but it won't solve all problems. The medications also wear off in late afternoon, which can lead to frustrations for the child and parents.

Children do test limits and that may have little to do with ADD. Also, your child may be stressed over academic or social problems apart from or secondary to the ADD. This situational emotional reaction may have little to do, at least directly, with ADD or with medication effects. If you see patterns of misbehavior in certain situations or at certain times of the day, discuss this with your doctor. Medications do wear off at different rates; there may need to be an adjustment.

Reader Question: Is my child likely to need medication right through high school and college, and maybe all his life?

The answer is "maybe." Each year you, your child and your doctor should review how the medication is going. Is there evidence of real improvement in terms of day to day functioning? If the answer is yes, I would be inclined to continue through the school years, including college. Don't forget, in college there is likely to be a heavy workload in terms of both quantity and level of difficulty. Also, there is a need for the child to be much more focused on lengthy lectures in college. The child needs to be much more independent and organized in college. The semester is short too, usually fifteen weeks not twenty as in high school. They need to do more work in less time. Medication may help in all these areas.

Medication can be used flexibly in college. I have many patients who have quite variable schedules in college. They may have a short workday with one class on some days and a super long workday with four classes and writing papers at night on another day. Many of these students take a shorter-acting medication once, twice or three times a day, depending upon their schedule.

Step 4: Consider long-term use

The question of how long medication should be used has been debated for many years. As noted above, through the 1980s the idea of children progressing into adulthood with their ADD issues was not even considered. Today it appears kind of silly to think ADD would magically disappear after age eighteen or so.

Medication in the adult years tends to vary. Hopefully the lower the severity of the ADD, the greater coping skills acquired, and the selection of an appropriate job and life style will help things all fall into place and there will be no need for medication. However, I have many adults who feel comfortable and more effective with daily medication. Some use it also for work only. Others use medication for special tasks and tests. It all depends on the individual circumstances such as the severity of their ADD, the challenges of work and family, the effectiveness of the medication, etc.

Reader Question: What if my young adult child feels he is doing fine and doesn't need medication anymore? Should I push the issue?

Your parenting job will never end, regardless of age. Being a parent gives you a license to offer an informed opinion. However, once that is shared, it's not your life. It is your adult child's decision to make, not just in medication areas, but also in terms of academic and vocational pursuits. You might try to listen to their objections regarding medication. They may have specific concerns, which should be raised with their doctor. They also may have a milder version of ADD and they may have sufficient coping skills to give it a try without medication. Always suggest a timetable, reassessing their functioning in a specific time frame, say six months or a year. You can easily go back to stimulant medications at any time with the same benefits as before.

Reader Question: I have heard that medications can dull emotions and creativity. Isn't that a problem for ADD children?

Stimulant medications have a wide range of effects beyond improving attention. It can quiet an active child and smooth out the emotional highs and lows. This may alarm some parents. I generally urge parents to stick with medications for a while, consulting often with the doctor. Many of these early side effects diminish over a short period of time. Dosage, timing, and type of medication may need to be changed.

Step 5: Consider medications other than stimulants

While stimulants are still the gold standard for treating ADD, if these are not tolerated by your child you might discuss alternative options with your child's doctor. Many children can benefit from an anti-depressant, for example. At relatively low doses these medications can greatly reduce anxiety associated with ADD.

Antihypertensive medications can reduce anxiety as well as angry outbursts. By reducing the emotional and behavioral problems often associated with attention issues, your child might be more amenable to behavioral management approaches and they might be more receptive to educational accommodations.

Your child's doctor may not wish to try various medications or he or she may be reluctant to combine stimulants with other medications. You can request a referral to a pediatric psychiatrist or pediatric neurologist who specializes in ADD issues.

Age appropriate collaboration

Any decision to even consider medication should involve your child's participation, at any age. By the time you get to considering medication, you have already thoroughly discussed the definition of ADD and their symptoms which support the diagnosis. You both may have completed some rating scales describing the symptoms of ADD. Your child probably has completed ADD testing. The use of medication as a possible treatment option should not be a big surprise at this point.

Parents may want to do some reading on medication options for ADD. There is a wide range of information on the internet about ADD medications. Check reliable and unbiased sources such as the magazine "ADDitude." Ask your pediatrician to recommend appropriate books on the subject. Be careful though as many articles and books may have a bias for or against medication. You may wish to share a few articles with an older child after reviewing them. For younger children, you can summarize a few points you have learned from your readings.

Your child can rate their pre-medication level of focusing (e.g., 1 to 10, 10 being maximum functioning) and post-medication level of focusing. They need to be aware of the approximate duration of the medication's effect as well, otherwise they may report little benefit, based on poor late day performance. It might be helpful for them to rate themselves at a few points during the day and early evening. Ask about the usual side effects too; i.e., appetite reduction and thirst. Parents often choose to start medication on a weekend to observe and monitor effects before use at school.

Objective data such as grades and reports from teachers will help us understand if the medication is having a positive effect on attention, as well as teachers' assessment of overall behavior. Many parents repeat a few subtests of their previous testing while their child is on medication, to look for objective signs of improvement with medication. Your pediatrician may ask parent and teachers to repeat the rating scales after a medication trial has been in place.

Reader Question: What if my child is improving by all measures but doesn't want to continue the medication?

There are a couple of reasons for such a response. One reason might be simple denial. They may not want to have the label or diagnosis of ADD. Some discussions and possibly some books aimed at children or teens might be helpful to build acceptance. Another reason might be they feel quiet, flat in emotion, and lacking in the energy and excitement compared with their pre-medication life. That is a bit tougher. Listen well and acknowledge there are some "good" aspects of ADD. It is nice to have an abundance of energy, be funny and a bit crazy in everyday life. The dulling effect of medication tends to wear after several weeks or months. Children also need to understand that significant improvements in their overall functioning may outweigh negative effects. They should be encouraged to discuss their feelings with you and with their pediatrician, openly, without criticism. Minor changes in dosage and timing can be helpful.

Question: Stimulant medication

a. Works quickly, first day, first dose
b. Has modest side effects usually managed easily
c. Can be used with older children and young adults
d. Works particularly well with hyperactive type ADD
e. Will not correct all problematic attitudes and behaviors
f. Can flatten mood and energy a bit in some hyperactive ADD children
g. All of the above

Dr. Leon Schofield

Chapter 5: Reward the Process, Not the Product

Process and product defined

Process refers to all of the steps necessary to arrive at an end point, the completion of the task. Process includes the initial thoughts and feelings. Process includes the planning. Process includes clarifying and learning more about what is required. Process means managing setbacks along the way. Process means setting small goals or milestones to mark progress. ADD children often struggle with all of these important elements of processing.

Product refers to the outcome of that effort. That product may be the homework that has been completed. The product may be the state of the room after cleaning. The product may be more social such as playing cooperatively or asking a question in class.

The problem with more traditional product-focused rewards

Rewards are routinely used by parents and teachers to help motivate a child to complete a task. Unfortunately we usually give rewards when the job is done. The problem for ADD children is that they often do not have the requisite processing skills to get to that goal. ADD children often have difficulty with:

- Understanding instructions
- Exaggerating the scope of the task and time needed
- Managing failures and frustrations during the task
- Failing to "self-reward" along the way
- Failing to appropriately seek help when they get stuck
- Failing to know when to end, quitting too early or obsessing too long

Therefore the rewards are often difficult or impossible to achieve for many ADD children. As a consequence of difficulty staying on task and finishing, ADD children often train their teachers and parents to expect less and do more for them. Partly out of impatience, partly out of sympathy, parents and teachers often reduce the expected work. They may give a reward anyway, for half the work done. They may even over-explain and demonstrate, eventually doing part of the work.

The problem with this common outcome is that the child has not learned coping skills. Without these coping skills, there will be little success down the road. All parties including parents, teachers, and the ADD child will come to expect less, when more may be possible. We may teach children how to use their problems to get others to work more. A better goal is to help your child to develop the coping strategies that will help him or her independently reach many goals.

Reader Question: That's a lot to think about. I generally see my child's resistance as a power play, not a coping strategy. Can it be both?

Sure. Your child will do what is necessary to avoid immediate distress. They are smart and will play any card available. They might try to play the sympathy card. "I'm stupid. I'm sad. I wish I was dead." Or they might just try wearing you down with fifteen-minute checks by you until late into the night. Eventually you will get tired and give up or lay down some crazy punishment like, "You are grounded for the rest of the year." They also may agree to give you just a little work, so that you will gradually accept less and less.

It is important to realize that resistance and manipulation are a lot of work on their part for very little payoff. There still will be a big cost to their resistance and avoidance in the near future. But the immediate avoidance of a difficult and stressful task takes precedence over some longer term negative outcome. Your child wants relief right now. They have little concern for the problems their resistance may cause a year later. You can use modest limits and sanctions, but put most of your effort into finding out the "real reasons" for the resistance.

Little good comes from a spiraling cycle of punishments and attacks. This teaches your child to use ever more extreme methods of resistance, and does not help him to learn good coping strategies. Let's look at a few ways to help your child learn good coping skills and to help your child learn to reward themselves for formulating and using these skills.

Step 1: Reward Initial Focusing

Before you even begin the instructions, make sure you have you child's full attention. Part of the reason children fail is that they often don't even hear much of the initial request or instruction. Make sure you get an affirmative verbal response such as, "Yes, I'm listening," before you even begin. Even if your child is listening, they still may misinterpret or misunderstand. But at least insure that they are beginning to listen.

Once you have achieved some effort to focus on your message, it's important to communicate what you want done specifically, along with how it should be done if possible. If the task has several parts, you likely will need to break it down step-by-step. Write it down. A visual list is better as a checklist than a mental checklist. With a physical list you can cross off each item with a big red pen. That's very satisfying for adults too! Remember the collaboration part. Have your child write the list if possible, post it and return it finished later. Have them consider the priorities. Teach your child to do the work.

If you see your child is making an effort to focus on the initial information or instructions, by repeating them, writing it down, asking questions, etc. offer verbal praise again citing specifics. With younger children, you may use stars or checks that can be accumulated for some rewards later. Be specific, e.g., "You looked right up when I started talking – three stars!" or "You wrote it down – great job!"

Step 2: Reward positive initial self-statements

Work on having a child express a positive attitude right out of the box. Start with asking them to come up with a positive self-statement about how they plan to clean their work area, how they will take a break after twenty minutes, how much work they will do in twenty minutes, how they will self-reward when they do a good job, and how they will handle likely frustration ahead.

Remind your child that negative words produce negative chemicals in our brain which do not help performance. Negative thoughts and words produce chemicals to help with "fight or flight." On the other hand, "I will do my best" or "OK, ready to go," sets the stage for more positive chemicals in our brains. Have your child come up with their own positive starting statements.

If you reward some good starting statements, mention the exact phrase or action that you observed that was helpful. You can't reinforce a specific behavior you have observed with a general statement. Be specific about what you want to see repeated. Don't say, "Good job getting ready." Do say, "It was great that you checked your book bag before you packed your lunch" or "Thanks for asking me to repeat what I said because you got busy and missed something."

If you notice your child got through a tough challenge, don't say, "Good job; you didn't give up." Do say, "I noticed you stopped and went on to the next problem when you got stuck. You also circled the number of the problem and wrote a marginal note, 'Come back to this.' That helped you finish – good job."

Step 3: Reward your child's controlling the visual field

We usually take in things with our eyes first. Most ADD children see everything, even small details that may not be relevant. Everything jumps up to their attention. Like a horse without blinders, they can't afford to see the whole world or they panic! Explain to your child how the ADD brain takes in too much information, without filtering it. Then the brain gets overwhelmed. It wants to shut down and run away. I often say to children, if your brain could do it, it would climb out of your ear and go for a walk.

Reward your child for reducing their visual world. Have them come up with a list of ways to accomplish this. The list may start with looking away, closing their eyes for a few seconds, putting clutter out of their visual line, folding their math homework sheet in half, putting an object that is pleasant and relaxing to look at on an otherwise clean desk surface, etc. Look at the walls where the child sleeps or does homework. Are they cluttered with too many pictures, memos and lists? Keep it simple and neat.

Reader Question: Wait a minute. You slipped in a "relaxing object" to be placed on their desk. I thought you wanted to reduce visual distraction. How would a relaxing object on the desk help? Wouldn't they just play with it?

That's a good point. A small picture, a sea shell, a ceramic figure, or a plastic flower are fine. They become part of the landscape. They don't call on us to play. Yet they provide in a glance, a message of calmness and safety. I have a couple of simple items like that on my desk. Kids do their testing without playing with the stuff. Parents say the office is pleasant and "homey." You don't want the "relaxing object" to be an electronic game, of course! If your child plays with the object, have a discussion about that and find something that will have less of a temptation to play with it. Let your child work on that. Then let them monitor how that worked out. Remember, you are the coach.

Also, on the visual stimulation front, use indirect lighting if possible. Overhead fluorescent lighting is too intense. It highlights everything. The light from a small desk lamp tends to help focus on things directly in front of them. Have your child inspect and improve their visual space. Again, reward with praise, checks or star if you wish – any effort to manage their visual space.

Step 4: Reward time management and setting mini-goals

ADD children often have poor sense of time. They can't accurately determine how much time is needed for a task. They may feel overwhelmed by what seems to you to be a very simple request. They may go in the opposite direction too and think the task is a breeze and can be done in a few minutes. ADD children don't estimate the time needed well. When they are in the middle of things, they also don't sense how much time has passed.

Help your child to break down tasks into smaller, more manageable parts, estimating how long each part of the job will take. Make sure the child has access to a clock for the desk, preferably one with a count-down alarm. This will allow them to estimate time needed for portions of the task, keeping a proper pace. Over time, with practice, your child will learn to judge the time needed for a task. Over time they will learn to pace themselves more appropriately.

Since most tasks are pretty lengthy, it is essential to set mini-goals. We know how ADD children dread unfinished work, piles of work, returning to endless tasks, etc. Virtually everything they do should include establishing a mini-goal with a short-term horizon. Ask your child what they can reasonably expect to do in fifteen minutes (for younger children) or thirty minutes (for older children). The goal needs to be as objective as possible; examples: "I will read ten pages. I will do two pages of math questions. I will write five pages of my report. I will sweep half of the garage floor."

The point of the mini-goal is to celebrate mini-successes in the longer path to the finish line. Feeling good about your effort is our best insurance to stay the course, for children or adults. Encourage your child to make appropriate estimates, to test these and to modify them as he or she goes along. As you coach along these lines, be sure to spot good efforts on their part to set and stick to the mini-goals.

Use verbal praise and be specific about what you are praising. For example, "good job with your mini-goals" may be too general. Be specific, such as, "I really like that you thought about the time it would take took to read a page, before estimating what you could do in thirty minutes for the homework." or "I like the way you put a sticky note on the page you expected to reach after thirty minutes of reading." or "I like that you set the timer right in front of you and checked it every five minutes or so as you did your work in order to keep up the pace."

Step 5: Reward better organizational management

It is crucial for you to address messy and disorganized work areas, not just the immediate desk surface noted above. You need to start with the basic principle that it's a lot easier to organize your stuff if you have less stuff. Try to encourage your child to discard anything they have not used in six months. Have a pile for recycle and a box for long term storage to give to their grandchildren when they are eighty. Actually, I'm kidding about that. There should be an annual spring cleaning of the long-term storage area with a goal of discarding at least a third of your "treasures." That's great advice for anyone, not just ADD children.

Things that are used on a nearly daily basis need to be placed in the most up-front and obvious places. Shelves, crates, vertical desktop file holders, etc., can hold more stuff without taking up too much space. There are plenty of storage options available at your local office supply store. Take your child on a field trip!

Reader Question: My child says he knows where everything is and says we shouldn't touch anything. It is really messy in there, sometimes with paper plates and Styrofoam cups. Should I just let him learn the hard way?

They are framing the mess as a personal choice. More than likely it is so overwhelming they don't know where to begin or how to proceed. Most children and most adults too, actually like things neat and organized. They just don't know how to make that happen easily. So, they claim it's fine and they like it that way.

You do have a right to insist on common health standards. You don't want the room condemned by the health department. You can do the typical parent thing and set minimum standards, enforcing it with a no electronics rule until it's done. There will be protests and inspections. You will end up doing half the work. However, they have not done any planning, execution or maintenance. They have learned nothing. It may take a bit longer, but as coach, you can help them actually learn to be better at organizing.

Step 6: Manage your own organizational task along with your child

You might simultaneously work on your own organizational project. This can be great modeling. Isn't it time you cleaned your closet, or the garage? Compare notes with your child often. Empathize with the difficulty of parting with things. Empathize with the struggle to decide where to put things. Model taking breaks. Model "feeling good" with part of the project completed. Try to keep work areas fairly uncluttered. Ask your child to critique your effort periodically. They may have a few suggestions to help you out.

The act of both of you working on similar tasks sends a powerful message. First, organization issues are for everyone, not just ADD children. Second, seeking advice and help is always a good idea. Third, things can be more fun when it's done with others. Make sure your child is doing the thinking and planning. You may start with a few general observations and suggestions, but back off quickly and let them do the work.

Step 7: Reward better management of failure and frustration

Parents need to let their child know that it's OK and it's even necessary to fail. They may see the task as hopeless at the first sign of failure or frustration. We all know the "I can't!" cry of the child as they put on a drama worthy of Macbeth. You can share examples of your own negativity in your childhood or you can share more recent negativity in your personal experiences at work or at home. Let your child know you got frustrated, made a bad choice, then you fixed it. Remind them they can and must learn to manage frustration and failure which are inevitable.

Most adults and children without ADD tend to manage failures better. They say "oops" or "darn" to themselves or they say it out loud. Then they fix it. If they can't fix it, they simply go to the next question or the next part of the task. They don't stop and remain stuck. They may ask for help. They may take a break and come back to it later. ADD children have difficulty with this. They have no tools to handle failure. Many ADD children will have anxiety just anticipating the task, expecting failure. The typical coping strategy for ADD children is to race through it with errors and finish it as fast as possible. Others can be more obsessive about it, pondering each small detail, never finishing.

Parents should explain the science of failure. All human brains are wired to respond with "fight or flight" when we are faced with danger. This is helpful for survival if there was true, real danger ahead. The problem is that some brains are more sensitive to danger than others, particularly ADD brains. There really isn't a life-threatening situation when a word is misspelled. You might share an example of your own recent past where you over-estimated the threat before you. Teach your child to use less emotionally charged terms, resorting to "Oops" or "Pickles!" when needed. Your child might prefer to rate their frustration on a scale. An older child might rate themselves, e.g., "I'm at a 8.38 on a 10 point scale." Notice there is a serious side – the stress is up. But there is a humorous side in the precision of the measurement of the stress, which in itself lowers the stress levels.

Your child needs to make a positive action when stuck. Having a cue word such as "pickles" may help to reduce the stress, particularly since it is neutral and even funny. More strategies may be needed to avoid the negativity pit. I suggest that a child frustrated with a school task circle the number and write a short phrase next to the tough question such as, "no clue … don't know … beats me … come back to this." In military parlance it's called a "fighting withdrawal" and it leaves the child feeling he is in command, not defeated. It is a choice to leave, not a retreat. Let your child develop their own system to avoid the feeling of defeat.

Step 8: Reward proper endings

Encourage your child to stop. It would seem this should be the easiest step. But ADD children often miss key parts of a task that may be obvious to others. They also may have a very different definition of "finished." As we have seen, most ADD children have a tendency to either race through things, or get stuck and obsess about it. ADD children can learn to put a time limit on their working, stopping and assessing it, rating the pros and cons of their work product

Adults usually screen and rate their child's work. Why can't ADD children learn to "grade" their own work? A task should not be complete without a self-check, whether it is a paper for school or cleaning their room. You should not be the probation officer looking behind every door and under the bed, or checking each line of a homework paper. You can rate your child's rating, of course. Your reinforcement is largely based on how thorough and accurate they were in their self-monitoring and self-rating of their own work and how they plan to fix it.

Step 9: Reward your child for self-rewarding

So far we see that the parent is doing most of the spotting of behaviors that work or don't work on the road to completing tasks. They have been good coaches, helping their child to try various approaches to master the journey to job completion. However, the job of a good coach is ultimately to work themselves out of a job. The same is true with parenting. Always keep in mind the real prize. Your chief goal is to have your child become a self-managing, well-adjusted adult. To that end, they must learn to coach themselves. Part of that coaching is learning to self-reward. They need to celebrate the small steps in order to get to the finish line.

A note on reward systems

Be sure to include your child in the setting up of your reward system. Agree on clear, objective and specific target behaviors you are reinforcing. Have your child make the chart with as little input on your part as possible. Post it in a convenient place. Have your child monitor and use the chart.

If you do want to try a reward system, vary the size and frequency of the rewards given as well as the timing of rewards. That can help the improvements generalize into everyday situations and settings. Charting everything is difficult and boring, as well as impractical. You are not going to run upstairs and mark every check you give. You can state, "You get two checks for hanging up your coat right away when you came home," adding, "You can go up now and put them on your chart, or we can keep a running total in our heads and put it on the chart after supper – your choice." On other occasions you may use just verbal praise and no checks. They may get 1, 2, 3 or no checks. Checks can be given for one or a few target behaviors, which also keeps them on their toes.

Different levels of reward may be offered (1, 2, 3 or 10 checks) depending upon the difficulty of the task. For example, I would offer big rewards for such things as quickness to recover from a failure or frustration, creating new coping strategies, or accurately spotting flaws or problems in their work without blowups or complaints. It's great to give a big payoff when you see a significant shift in their taking greater responsibility and ownership in the problem and its solution. Parents might say "That was great that you found your mistake, took a breath, circled the number and went on — seven checks for that!"

It is impossible to give an exact amount of checks or stars for each bit of behavior exhibited that focuses on a few target behaviors. That would become stressful and unpleasant for you and for your child. Explain to your child that you would rather give variable checks, occasionally giving several, not just one every time and sometimes just giving verbal praise. Explain to your child that this system is the best way to learn and maintain new habits. It's true and you can quote me on that, literally.

Reader Question: What about the old-fashioned reward system? Shouldn't a child get a reward for completing the task not just the process?

I have no problem with an acknowledgement of an achievement, verbally and perhaps with checks or stars. However, the key to success is going to be learning the processing skills that will produce the success. That is the message we want to send to our children too. That message is sent when you put your focus and your rewards on the process, not product.

Age appropriate collaboration

Younger children will need more guidance, of course. They will have less capacity to manage themselves as they work, compared with older children. You will likely have to start with some specific processing behaviors you believe will be helpful.

You will need to prime the pump a bit by offering a few suggestions such as, "Here are a few options. Which plan sounds best for you?" Ask them to think about it before deciding, and ask them to offer reasons for any preferred action. The goal is to get them to begin to think critically and independently. You will have to break down any planning into several phases. Remind them to start with a planning step, i.e. thinking about the problem for a while and deciding what they will need, how they will start, what steps they can take, when they will likely need a break, etc. Always think before acting. ADD children often forget this. Help your young ADD child by taking notes and reviewing them out loud a few times to make sure you both are "on track." You are modeling good coping strategies.

Younger children will need to break down tasks into very small pieces and they will need more frequent praise and reward. Remember their understanding of time is different than time for older children and adults. An hour is forever for a seven year old. A simple task seems like a mountain to them. They also tire more quickly than older children. Breaking every task down into small bites makes it all more manageable.

Older children have stronger language skills. They are likely to need less direction and less support. However, don't forget that ADD children are immature in their thinking and in their expectations. They tend to over-reach, leaving them vulnerable to failure and frustration. Encourage small steps and frequent self-rewards. Older children want to be more independent and you can use this to help them take better charge of their life. They still will need some coaching and cheerleading. Remind them that you too need to have objective input from others and that you also feel good when progress is made on a project. You too enjoy celebrating a partial success with self-praise, a break, or a little reward such as coffee or a walk. Share a few personal experiences along these lines.

Have older children think about how to approach a problem while you take notes. Writing steps, lists and calendars can be difficult for many ADD children and writing can distract them from the real process of thinking and planning. Don't be judgmental at this point. Let them brainstorm. You can examine the details after they have a good general framework about the task. Then you can ask for more details or clarification, prompting them to narrow down on the more difficult parts. For example, you might ask, "Can you give more details about that? It's still too general."

With or without a reward system, it's important to celebrate small victories. Think about a spontaneous lunch break at a nice restaurant or an ice cream at the local shop as a way to recognize a breakthrough. That breakthrough should be a major self-discovered improvement in coping strategies, a new way they have found to manage stress, improved self-reward or a thorough checking and revision of their own work, without prompting by parents.

Remember the goal of rewards is to encourage the thoughts and behaviors that keep your child in the game and that keep your child moving forward even in the face of difficulty. The final **product** is important, but you will never get there if you don't learn to persevere. Reward **process** mostly.

Question: ADD children need to reward process, not product because:

    a. Learning to prepare for a task is important.

    b. Having a positive attitude improves the probability of success.

    c. Self-rewarding during a task helps to stay focused.

    d. Managing failures and frustrations along the way is essential.

    e. All of the above

Dr. Leon Schofield

Chapter 6: Use Humor

Why humor works

Very little is written about the healing power of humor in the treatment of ADD. We know that humor touches us in powerful ways. Humor releases chemicals in the brain that improve our mood while we face difficult problems. These positive chemicals help us to "stay in the game" and keep working on solutions. Without humor we tend to slide into catastrophizing which drives parents to try to control and fix problems immediately. ADD children will rebel and resist such attempts to control and fix things.

Humor can be a healing force for ADD children and their parents. Humor helps us to forgive our child and ourselves. Humor helps us to accept our flaws as a normal part of life. Humor helps us to bond with our child. Humor helps us to approach and communicate with others in similar predicaments.

Humor and exaggeration can be used at all phases of diagnosing and treating ADD. It can help your child see their problems objectively, see the need for trying new strategies, accept the difficult path of self-management, and be open to changing these strategies over time as circumstances and demands change. Humor is an excellent addition to your ADD tool box.

Step 1: Overcome your obstacles to the use of humor

The biggest obstacle to the use of humor is the attitude that using humor to address any problem is not politically correct. Unfortunately this attitude can take a very valuable treatment tool off the table, as you will see. As long as humor is not used to demean any individual or any group, humor can and should be used as often as needed. Another related obstacle to the use of humor is that humor may trivialize a problem. On the contrary, humor is needed for the more serious problems individuals, families, groups or countries face.

Another objection to humor may be that it is irreversible. Once you go down the "make it light" path, you can't return. That is not true. In fact, humor should be a free-flowing two-way highway, where you can move to the light side and then to the serious, back and forth, freely, as needed. Humor needs to be used flexibly, with no hard rules.

A final objection may be that few can use humor. We all know how awkward it can be to try to tell a joke, only to have it fall flat because of a detail left out or because of bad timing by not inserting the right pauses in the right place. While this objection may be true for stage comics, it is not relevant to the ADD issues presented here. The humor we address is observational. No specific skill sets are needed other than a willingness to share personal observations and a willingness to seek input of a similar nature from your child. Children do have a pretty good sense of humor naturally, but that tends to be squelched a bit over the years in all of us.

Step 2: Discuss with your child the benefits of humor and exaggeration

Your child may not see the humor in everyday life, especially their own life. Explain that humor helps us to keep things lighter, and not get burdened by problems in life. Explain how you use humor to laugh a bit at your own attitudes and behaviors. Remind them that comedians on TV help us face tough problems by making us laugh about those problems.

Give your child a specific example of something dumb that you did. Your stubbornness or carelessness or rushing may have contributed or caused a bigger problem. You may want to use the phrase "What could go wrong?" repeatedly. That phrase sums up our tendency to want things our way, to pursue them, and to insist on having it our way in spite of obvious risks and problems. Ask your child to contribute an example of a "What could go wrong moment" in their past.

We humans tend to exaggerate to make a point. By exaggerating something to a ridiculous level, it immediately reduces the reactive emotions that arise. To say our life is over because we struck out at the ball game, we can see the silliness of that. It's not really that important. A child I met recently appeared to get upset and almost panicky every time he made a mistake. I suggested he needed to coach himself, with a little humor. I suggested he say "I'm doomed!" every time he made a mistake. He laughed, of course, seeing the ridiculousness of this exaggerated description of his state. He used it regularly thereafter, and it stopped his tendency to view any failure or frustration as a disaster.

Give an example of how you have looked at some recent event as a huge disaster, only to see it was not a big deal. Make the case for unloading emotions through exaggeration. If they get into the absurdity of their own drama, they will be able to reduce the negative emotions quickly. Encourage them to use words like "disaster" and "doomed."

Step 3: Laugh at your bad habits and "tragedies"

We have suggested parents do some self-disclosure already. Let's discuss this in more specific terms. You can jump in anytime with a funny story about your own mistakes. Children love to hear of adult misfortune. If you feel your child is quite sensitive about a topic you are about to address, you might start right out with a personal story of a related nature. You don't need any big explanation. Just start out with, "I want to tell you about something I did at your age which you might find funny."

The story should have a nice build-up, providing details on the setting and circumstances of your disaster. Even more importantly, share your inner thoughts at the time. Share the "What-could-possibly-go-wrong" thoughts. Share the catastrophe you expected that didn't happen. Ask your child what they think is the moral or lesson learned. Discuss it and then bring it into your child's immediate problem.

Being able to acknowledge our shortcomings reduces stress over these behaviors. It helps us avoid excuses and blaming others. We all have characteristics and habits that we aren't too proud of. We may have to argue to prove a point. We may have to talk fast to dominate the conversation. We may have to offer many excuses. We may simply say we have done something perfectly when we haven't. We may do things super slowly to avoid mistakes. We may rush things to get them over with. Nobody is perfect. We can and should try to avoid mistakes and reduce our bad habits.

Explore with your child their bad habits. Ask them to tell you a couple of their bad habits. Ask them what tricks they have used or tried to reduce or change these habits. Explore other things they can say to themselves, coach themselves, when the situation comes up again. Going away is often the simplest coping option. Lingering in a place of irritation or in a place of temptation will lead to trouble. Sometimes you just have to make a retreat.

Step 4: Decide when to use humor

Humor is helpful in many situations. ADD children are not particularly socially aware. ADD children should use humor in a limited set of circumstance. They can usually use humor safely when it is self-directed. Exaggeration is the easiest to use. A child might say, "I have so much homework I will have to stay in my room until Christmas." or "I have to wait so long in line that I may have to take a nap." or "I messed up so bad I will have to live in the garage this winter."

I would discourage trying to use physical humor, especially for hyperactive ADD children. We don't want them to become class clowns. They probably already do a good job of that.

Humor can be helpful especially dealing with a stubborn or chronic problem. The reason for being stuck and unable to change is often a tendency to catastrophize with a grave interpretation of events, along with a sense of helplessness to manage. Humor can help put things in better perspective. It can encourage more flexibility and willingness to take some risks to change. For example, a child might say, "If I ever remember to pick up my clothes, I will get a trophy." or "I may need to tie a tin can around my neck to remind me to take home my math homework." Making a small joke helps to plant the action or activity we need to do prominently in our brains.

A pending problem can also produce defensiveness and poor coping. If a child sees some major obstacle ahead, the anticipation of the event can produce massive defensiveness well before the event or situation. Humor can help open the door to discussion about coping strategies. It can allow a child to experiment with these coping strategies, not just run away. For example, "If I go to that big family party, I may have to hide under the couch. Can you hand me a cookie every hour or so?"

Reader Question: OK, I can see the usefulness of humor. What if I'm not in the mood for humor I'm just angry. I don't think I would be a good teacher about how to use humor at that time.

On the contrary, that's the perfect time. Use humor to deal with your own mood issues, right there on the spot. You can start with the exaggeration, e.g., "I'm so angry I could eat that tree over there." A little silliness helps too. It forces the child's mind to step out of straight-line thinking path, and consider the ridiculousness, yet the appropriateness. Then you can move on to managing the anger, e.g., "Counting to three is not going to cut it. I'm so angry I should count backwards from a hundred in Spanish. Wait, I don't know Spanish. I'll just have to count the number of dots in the ceiling tiles." Then a more normal action might be considered to reduce tensions, such as building with Legos for a while or reading a comic book. Venting some of the stress with humor makes it more possible to find a realistic coping strategy.

Humor may not solve a problem, but it helps reduce the tension and therefor humor helps us be more open to talking about the problem and about managing the problem. With humor the temperature is down, and both sides have disarmed. We are closer to solving problems.

Step 5: Lighten up the environment

We already have discussed the benefits of having less cluttered surroundings. Here I would add that there should be some pictures or objects in our space that connote happiness and pleasure. They may be a poster, picture or special toy. Maybe it is a cartoon, joke or saying that inspires us or helps us to laugh a little. There are calendars that also bring some joy to the room. Talk with your child about what minor changes can be made to make his or her room more of a happy place.

Reader Question: My child wants to make faces and fart. He likes to tease his brother too. Is that funny? Not to me. He just wants attention.

I agree. That is not humor. Discuss why that is not appropriate humor. It distracts others. There is no real joke to it. Try to discuss ways your child might tone it down a few notches. Discuss when it might be a good time to try humor. Certainly, it would not be in the middle of a class lesson.

Final words

Humor cannot be mean-spirited or attacking. Your child needs to know we are not laughing at him or her. Humor has to be delivered with a spirit of love, not rejection. It must be delivered with empathy. It will work well when you can use it to reveal your own limitations and problems. Humor must be encouraging and supportive. It must be aimed at universal themes of frustration and worry. If attempts at humor are met with resistance or irritation, even after a discussion of the merits of humor, leave it at the side of the road for now. Revisit the topic at a later time, perhaps when there is less situational stress.

Explain how humor helps make problems more manageable. Discuss the importance of taking a lighter side to self-examination. Explain that humor is another secret weapon used by children and adults to cope better. Remember too that humor reduces chemicals in our brain that push us to "fight or flight," and humor helps us to produce more chemicals in our brains that make us happy

We all recall a certain cartoon character about a young child and his stuffed toy tiger. There is a unique side to ADD. The world is a very different place for children, especially for those with ADD. It's okay to have a chuckle about the plans and problems faced by children, with or without ADD. Reading some of Calvin's adventures might enlighten us and help us to relax just a bit, and that can open us all, children and adults, to change.

Age appropriate collaboration

It probably seems like humor is really not much of a big deal. How can humor really make a dent in the broad and serious problems of ADD? The lighter touch is helpful since it makes it possible to look more realistically at a problem and since it makes starting the work of coping easier and achievable. It also is great for parents who tend to drift towards the catastrophizing view of ADD.

Younger children are naturally more inclined to understand humor and to use humor. A more physical type of humor works well with younger children. Children are likely to see humor in imagining their school books attacking them in their sleep. They may actually sing a silly song before starting each math assignment. They might put on a Superman cape before starting their homework. They might enjoy reporting their thoughts and feelings through a sock puppet.

Older children will tend to resist humor. They will likely want to look at more internal self-talk humor. Sarcasm works well with this group. Ask them to think about what their definition of funny is and how that would apply to the current stressful situation.

Question: Humor is helpful in working with ADD children because it:

    a. Helps the child be more open to owning and changing a problem
    b. Reduces the stress chemicals in the body
    c. Reduces the catastrophizing that children and parents tend to do
    d. Opens up creative solutions
    e. All of the above

Chapter 7: Use Limited Punishment

What's wrong with punishment?

Observation of ADD children indicate they are punished and they are given negative verbal comments far more than their non-ADD peers at school and at home. In spite of this excessive punishment and criticism, the skills and behavior of ADD children often remain poor. Punishment, just like rewards for product, don't work well for ADD children. If a child lacks good coping skills, both rewards and punishments will not be very helpful. Punishments and criticism seem arbitrary and unfair to the ADD child. They may see the goals and demands as impossible. Punishment may increase the risk of angry, oppositional behavior. Here are some valuable steps that can change your punishment practices and put you and your child on a more effective course.

Step 1: Don't act immediately, use a brief timeout

This is a very hard sell, I know. Misbehavior or disruptive behavior is seriously annoying and it often arouses a call for immediate and hostile response on your part. Take the time to evaluate before acting. You can certainly express disappointment, confusion or irritation. These are natural emotional responses to many situations. State that you and your child need a timeout to think about what just happened and what can be done about it. Remind them that the issue is not dead or avoided, just postponed for a short time.

Reader Question: What's wrong with reacting with a swift punishment? I don't see any down side to that. The child misbehaved and then there are the consequences.

That often works well with most children. But if we are dealing with ADD children who lack a certain measure of capacity to listen, recall, sustain attention, work through failure and complete a task, then you might be missing the point. They will see, somewhat correctly, adults as a punishment machine, arbitrarily lashing out at children for little reason and for actions they can't control. This encourages hostility towards authority figures, as well as promoting resistance to the oppressor, you.

I would rather have a child investigate the problem, identify possible reasons for failure, develop a corrective plan, and achieve success. There can be some postponement or suspension of free time activities during this critical time of reflection and planning. But I don't see that as punishment. It is problem solving. Once a problem has been investigated and solved, you can move on. There is no arbitrary and long punishment here. Think of the modeling you are doing. You think and plan before acting out angrily. This demonstrates a useful skill to the child. I know you are skeptical, but consider all the steps below.

Step 2: Avoid moral outrage

Parents tend to moralize as well as punish. "What's wrong with you! You know you shouldn't have eaten all the cookies." ADD children may steal toys, money or games from other kids or from the store. They may shout out angry insults and threats to family or friends when frustrated. Parents typically start right out of the gate with a severe, negative moral judgment. It doesn't work since the only actions you can get from your child is an agreement that they are indeed morally bankrupt and unworthy to be in the family. Or your child can attack the premise of your judgment, blame others, or simply yell and throw stuff to distract and control the argument. Not a good outcome.

So why do we do it? Parents are often morally outraged. They are also fearful. Seeing your child on a downward spiral invites you to project even bigger problems in the years ahead. Seeing the downward projection of this behavior likely will lead to your child becoming another Charles Manson in your mind. Parents also are likely to be embarrassed, since it is true that others often see the child's behavior problems as due to poor parenting. So, big lapses in judgment may light your fire!

Whatever you do, stop and cool off. Announce that you need to step away and cool off first before discussing it. That's great modeling. Ask them to reflect on how that happened, while you do the same. Returning to the discussion, now try to relate your concerns in a neutral, calm manner. You are here to gather information, not condemn. Remind them that most kids, especially those with ADD, often have trouble with impulsiveness and management of their emotions. Everyone must learn to walk away and avoid acting in a way that makes others angry or hurt or mistrustful of you.

Step 3: Work on strategies to immediately reduce reactive emotion

Your ADD child needs be aware that they need to work on managing their emotions first, and then work on the behavior and the solution. There is no solution without emotional control. So, the first step in this alternative approach to punishment is to learn to master emotions. Parents often misunderstand this. They want an immediate apology, an appreciation of the difficulty their child has created and a plan to fix it. That's way too premature. Manage emotions first.

Your child's emotions can be managed by walking away or looking away, literally or figuratively. Also, have your child take a few breaths. Your child can also replace negative thoughts with other mental activities such as reading, building with blocks, playing with toys, etc. Explain that this distracts your mind and puts you in a more relaxing place. Have your child think about and come up with their own list of mental or physical actions they can take to cool off.

Walking away seems to be hard for most kids. There is often the sense that you have been defeated. I recommend the "fighting withdrawal" method. If it's a temptation issue, they can say to themselves and parents, "I really want that but not now." or "Nope." or "Not now." Keep it short and simple and let them modify or make up their own script. If it is anger at someone they feel has been unfair or attacking, they can state, "I want to yell about this, but I need to cool off." or "I could fight about this, but I won't."

The second thing that your child can do is to immediately get busy doing something else to occupy their brain, focusing on that, instead of focusing on the temptation or on the offending agent. You probably have a truck-full of examples of how you have to do that at work. Share your own thoughts about how hard that is to do. Tie your shoes, get a drink of water, or go to the bathroom. Do something that requires your attention and that will help you pull away from the angry edge.

Step 4: Manage your own emotions

Excessive emotions on the part of your child will bring out excessive emotions in you. The standard parental reaction is an equal or greater display of emotion on your part and then the standard timeout. This is usually given, however, with a good dose of moralizing ("How could you say that; it was so rude!") and guilt-producing verbal attack ("I don't believe you could say that to your mother!"). After all, your emotions are now charged too. Try to not, once again, go too far down that road. Remind your child that you are working at formulating a calmer response. This is a good opportunity to model pulling away from the edge. Remind them too that their strong emotions set off others, including yourself, but that we all have to work at slowing that emotional roller coaster.

You might also use humor and exaggeration here. You might reflect that your fear is that if they don't pick up their dirty clothes every day, they will end up living in a box on the streets. But that probably isn't going to happen. Explain that parents project a problem in the present well into a catastrophe in the future. That's what parents do and that's why they blow up often. You can see the modeling effect going on here.

Reader Question: You keep mentioning "walk away." My child can't do that in school. My child can't even do that at home. If I am mad, I will really explode if my child gets up and walks away. How do they "walk away"?

You are right about that. Even looking away signals disrespect. The look away or walk away idea is mostly for preventing stewing over this incident for a prolonged period after a brief exchange. If the child is right at the confrontational stage you described above, you need to educate your child on ways they can let their brains turn away if not the body. Let your child puzzle over this dilemma. Thinking calming thoughts helps.

Talking or coaching yourself can help. Taking a few deep breathes helps. They might come up with some creative options too. Perhaps some self-talk can work here such as, "OK, I can fix it." or "Let them yell; they'll cool off soon." or "Stay focused here; listen-up brain." If that doesn't work and your child feels they are at the brink of a meltdown, they might need other tactics.

Your child might try looking in the direction of the lecturing teacher or parent, but focus on a target behind them or just over the shoulder or head. They can also state that they are too upset to listen right now, asking for a quiet timeout before the details of the problem are discussed. Be empathetic. It really is hard for all of us to be criticized without becoming defensive, child or adult.

Step 5: Teach your child to make amends

A major deficiency of punishment in general is that it does not encourage making amends for the behavior problem. Once the punishment is served, it's over. There is no reflection on the damage done, no chance to address the broken relationship with peers or adults. In addition to learning new ways to fix a problem, children need to be able to offer amends to others they have hurt or inconvenienced. This can take the form of repairing, rebuilding or replacing physical damage, or by doing chores and tasks to pay for such damage. More importantly, it can be an offer of service to help in any way, another person who they have harmed by words or deeds. You can't fix some things, but offering to help is a great start to mending broken bonds. Making amends also heals the perpetrator, in this case, the ADD child. Making amends can raise their damaged self-esteem and help your child to see the possibility of redemption and hope.

Reader Question: Isn't that last statement a bit exaggerated? Children are used to punishment. They don't necessarily feel they have damaged their relationships. They don't feel hopeless. They probably expect punishment from time to time. It's just part of life.

It may be a touch melodramatic, but not by much. Let's not forget, ADD children get way more negative feedback, as well as way more punishment, compared with non-ADD children. They often do see themselves in a negative, downward spiral. They often do attribute their sometimes over-the-top behavior as a sign of some demon-like seed in them. This self-awareness may promote more negative actions on their part along with a feeling that they are powerless to change.

Our parenting goal should be to make punishment obsolete and unnecessary. That will never be completely achieved but we should strive to teach, not just punish. The punishments here are primarily brief, more of a timeout. Discussions center on investigating, understanding, finding alternative behaviors and choices, fixing things and making amends. If your child is an active participant in this process and has some good ideas and insights, a parole or probation may be in order!

Step 6: Consider probation or parole

Let's talk about probation, or parole. Even criminals get a second chance. After you have cooled off, you may want to discuss probation or parole, for "good" behavior. Good is defined a little differently. It's not just having a period of cooling-off, it is more like working at self-examination, self-awareness, exploring triggers for emotions and behavior and considering better ways to manage. If there is modest movement in these directions after the timeout or even well into a more extended period of isolation or punishment, you might consider probation or parole.

Like real probation or parole, there must be some work on the part of the child to recognize the nature of their "crime," what triggered it, and a plan of action to help monitor and control the problem in the future. For example, if the problem involved an overly emotional blowup, make sure that there are some specific coping strategies identified and practiced for the future when your child is faced with a challenge. If there was some impulsive incident – for example, taking something – there needs to be a specific management plan your child has proposed for the future. Perhaps that plan can include a script or comment they can use to create mental and physical distance between themselves and their temptation.

The management of failure or frustration and the management of blowups and meltdowns are addressed in greater depth in future chapters. But for now, just consider the possibility of granting parole or probation when you see evidence of good work on self-management. Be sure to label that specific example of good work when you grant this reprieve. For example, you can state, "It sounds like you figured out what triggered your behavior and you have thought about ways to change that in the future." Then you can offer the parole or probation.

Age appropriate collaboration

Younger children may need a bit more prompting to help them to think and reason, with respect to the problem behavior. They understand timeouts and removal of privileges. What they don't get is how they can change the outcomes for similar situations in the future. They simply want to serve their time and move on. Don't fall for that. Insist that they can think and reason and come up with reasons for both their negative emotions and inappropriate behaviors being triggered. Insist that they can come up with coping strategies that can improve the outcome in similar situations they will face in the future.

Older children are pretty articulate, but they will also try to blame others, offer excuses or apologize to get you to go away. They will offer general solutions such as "I will ignore them in the future." or "I will just walk away next time I am tempted." Push for specific mental scripts they will use to manage their emotions and actions. Push for preventative actions they will consider in the future to avoid confrontations or temptations. Push for "emergency plans" or "exit ramps" they might construct to handle a situation that may be distressing at home, school, sports event or family activity.

Question: Punishment doesn't seem to work very well because ADD children have:

    a.   Difficulty with delay of gratification
    b.   Difficulty with seeing what is expected
    c.   Difficulty with excessive reactive emotions
    d.   Difficulty with completing the goal or task
    e.   All of the above

Dr. Leon Schofield

Chapter 8: Move and Exercise

Coping with ADD in a sedentary world

In the "good old days," children often had a half-hour of recess and played outside every morning. They also often had thirty minutes for lunch, again with some opportunities for exercise and socializing. Today, there is such an emphasis on cramming as much academics as possible into the day that there is little time for physical exercise or socializing, even in elementary school.

In today's schools, the ADD child struggles without these breaks. Physical and mental breaks allow the brain to "defrag" itself and reset for the next task. The absence of such mental and physical breaks can adversely affect ADD children of both types to a greater degree than the general student population. I often tell parents, movement is good for all of us. The changing of our visual and auditory perspective as we exercise is itself a benefit.

Movement is the hallmark of hyperactive ADD children. While others may see movement as "off-task," for most hyperactive ADD children, modest movement actually improves their attention. That's not so crazy when you consider that children and adults without ADD often are physically busy in their deepest thoughts. They are likely to tap, rub their chins, and even pace. Many ADD children need to have physical movement simply to stay on task, not just for "deep thinking" about a problem.

Exercise seems to improve attention for short stretches of time. The reasons may be complex. I suspect some of this improvement may be due the fact that the brain has focused on the physical activity and put aside the information and emotions that occurred earlier, effectively rebooting the brain. Repetition and exercises are mundane and not stressful, though they require our attention. This might ready us for new information. Some of the improvement might even be due to the positive chemical changes produced by aerobic exercise. Whatever the reason, exercise is often beneficial.

Step 1: Enlist teachers to step up physical activity for your child

Parents should ask their child's teacher to provide activity and movement in the class. This may be done by having the child assist with tasks such as passing out papers, running an errand and cleaning the board. It would help too if the ADD child got up and brought their worksheets to the teacher's desk after a few minutes. Besides giving the child an opportunity to move around, getting up to show work to the teacher can give the teacher information on how well your child understood the task and it will indicate how quickly it is being done. It will also encourage your ADD child to break tasks down into smaller parts, in addition to encouraging them to seek feedback.

Many schools allow children to have cushions for seats which help them move a bit, allowing **a** rocking sensation without being disruptive to others nearby. Teachers may also allow or encourage a child to kneel in their chair or to sit with legs crossed under them. Some schools provide standing desks at the rear or side of the classroom. Schools may also suggest using a small ball for your child to squeeze in their pocket.

Reader Question: Won't that rocking on a cushion or squeezing a ball be distracting to other kids?

Generally, children are not distracted by such accommodations. Schools today are fairly active places. Children move their desks, get up, work on computers, walk to get a drink of water or sharpen their pencils, etc. There is a lot of activity in most classes. Minor movements by our ADD children will not be a problem. Of course, bouncing the ball or throwing it would not work well. There may need to be other accommodations in these cases.

Step 2: Help your child find discreet ways to move

Before beginning a discussion with your child about small movements that are normal and not disruptive, be sure to rule out some movements that are disruptive. I joke with children that standing on their desks doing jumping jacks would likely be frowned upon. Tapping your desk or kicking the chair I front of you wouldn't work either. The focus here is to help your child notice what the norm around them is, and what would cross the line. Teach your child to move about discreetly.

I suggest to children with either type of ADD, that when they find themselves off-task to use subtle movement. They can stretch the arms downward or forward under their desks. They can lean down and tie their shoes. They can roll their pencils in their hands slowly. They can reach down and grab their chairs, pulling upward in an isometric exercise. They can even simply lean forward. As they practice this, I have the child notice how that simple movement changes their visual perspective and wakes up their brains to take in the changes observed. This applies to desk work too. Tipping your head, moving the page an inch to the right, adjusting your pencil, all take brain activity and all help to alert and awaken the brain.

Some children prefer to not use the props schools offer (e.g., standing desks, cushions, squeeze balls) due to feeling embarrassed about needing them. Teaching them to use the above method of more subtle movement may work best. You may also try a more regularly scheduled discreet workout in class. They can identify a subject or time of day where drifting or leaping away mentally is a big problem.

This subtle workout activity should be planned and followed daily, e.g., right after completing a math sheet or writing exercise. Like anything, after we practice something several times it gets to be a habit. Start with some stretching motions, upper body and lower. The arms can be extended slowly, under the desk or at their sides. The legs can be stretched as well, under the desk. As with any exercise, stretch for several seconds, then relax.

After a brief stretching warm-up, your child may move on to squeezing shoulder blades slowly together or using the squeeze ball. I find that children like to do toe-pushups too. They can press their toes upward within their shoes, hold it for five seconds, then release. Finger stretching, generally in their laps, can also be helpful, particularly for ADD children who have difficulty writing. They tend to grip pencils tightly and often tire. As they tire, their writing can quickly become sloppy. The isometric chair lift noted above, can be done as part of this workout. Finish the workout with a "cool down;" i.e., stretching again. All of this can be done quickly in a few minutes and subtly without distracting others.

Reader Question: Hold on there. Even these small movements might be disruptive to kids and teacher. Doesn't the teacher want kids to settle down and sit quietly?

That is a risk. I practice with children doing each activity with minimal movement. For most ADD children, this type of exercise is far less disruptive than their normal behavior. A brief exercise routine might take just a few minutes. Even a short exercise routine of only a few minutes that can be a help for hyperactive ADD children. Working on subtle movement helps also to convey an attitude of self-control and self-management. It also suggests that there is nothing wrong with the need for activity, but it has to be managed properly.

Step 3: Encourage your child to ask for breaks

ADD children, both types, tend to ignore their need for movement. The will sit for so long, then mentally leave the room. Eventually many ADD children, especially the hyperactive ADD children, might become disruptive. I would recommend that ADD children regularly monitor themselves, looking for cues that they are getting bored and restless. They can ask to get a drink of water, or to go to the bathroom. This will only work a few times per day. They can decide what class or time of day that such a break might be needed most.

This further suggests to your child that they are responsible for managing their ADD. They need to be more proactive.

Step 4: Consider sports

Sports can be a mixed bag for younger children. Many ADD children of either type, do not work out well in team sports. That should not be surprising given the need for listening, taking turns, sitting, following rules, handling failure and frustration, dealing with peer and adult pressure, etc. Many sports have a lot of bench time, with little physical exercise. Some sports such as soccer offer fairly vigorous workouts to many at the same time. If your child's ADD is mild enough to allow your child to pay attention to the coach, he or she might derive some attention and social benefits from sports.

I have seen many young children, adolescent and young adult patients who have been involved in regular, active sporting activities. Many of them have done fairly well managing their ADD over the years. The child most likely to benefit from sports is likely to be a child with strong natural talents in that sport. Older children often report they feel much more focused for an hour or two after aerobic exercise. I have seen enough of this to conclude that there are likely true attention benefits with rigorous exercise. Younger children get some exercise in the playground, but the really rigorous exercise programs are usually found in middle and high school sports.

Individual sports tend to work better for many ADD children. Some may enjoy swimming, tennis, wrestling, skiing, etc. There tends to be more activity and less bench time.

Step 5: Consider non-sports activities

If your ADD child is not sports minded, individual exercise can still be done regularly. A brief daily workout on the treadmill might start the day well. Walking, jogging or biking vigorously can be helpful. Many ADD children can use a treadmill safely. Watch out for weight training. Younger children are not able to do this safely. Talk with your pediatrician about appropriate exercise.

While kids often prefer to isolate themselves in the game world, setting time for physical activity is a good idea for everyone. An exercise time each day, for you as well as for your children, can be a good habit to get into. If adults don't model healthy exercise it won't happen for their children, ADD or otherwise.

Great idea, but what if my inattentive ADD child has no interest in any kind of exercise, even if it's dressed up as "fun?" Should I force the matter?

Should you force good dental health and sleep habits? Of course, you should. Exercise is just part of that healthy picture. You should have a discussion about the value of this, acknowledging to your child that this is likely to be a hard sell. You can add that it's easy for you too to become a slave to TV or games. Have your child suggest some options that might appeal to you both. Look into programs at the local Y or community center, then you don't have to worry about setting it up or designing some healthy activity.

There's value in looking at books in the library and looking up information about your activity or in doing your research on the internet together with your child. You can find and develop an activity or hobby from such research. You may find books on hiking, biking, nature, camping, orienteering, etc., to be interesting. You can begin to learn about the world beyond the TV and games. You can plan a hike in your area. You can discuss and research what you might take along on your trip to the "wilderness." The advantage to the do it yourself approach (versus a preplanned program at the community center) is that it models searching for interests, designing your own activities, finding the necessary resources for your mission, planning it out and executing it without a big group and without a leader. This builds self-reliance and self-sufficiency.

Physical activity is very important, but we shouldn't forget mental activity as well. I would certainly encourage a child to learn chess, photography, cartooning, drawing, writing, etc., through individual or small group classes or workshops.

Reader Question: How about exercise in place at home like you may use in class? Are there home situations that might require some exercise in place?

Anytime your child needs to sit for a while, that can be an opportunity for that kind of exercise. Exercise in place might be at the dinner table waiting to be served, or sitting in a movie theater, or driving to the supermarket, or standing in line at the cash register, or watching a TV program as a family. Exercise! There is no need for special equipment!

Age appropriate collaboration

The world of young children is very different from that of older children. Younger children have to sit at the same desk and be with the same teacher most of the school day. Younger children also are more naturally active. On the positive side, there usually is some tolerance for activity in elementary grades. There usually is a lot of hands-on work, even if it is a difficult worksheet. There is usually an opportunity for more movement, walking around in the class, joining a work group, passing out papers, etc. Children understand the need for movement, so it's not a hard sell.

Older children will not opt for anything that calls attention to themselves. The subtle exercises at their desk might be acceptable for many older children, but squeeze balls, cushions, and standing desks aren't likely to fly for these kids. Older children also have the benefit of getting up every fifty minutes or so to go to their lockers and the next class. They may also have sports, clubs and activities that are more physical.

As older children develop hobbies and interests that have a strong physical activity component, they may also be finding outlets for themselves as adults. Hiking, biking, running, tennis, etc., don't require a lot of equipment or money. These non-team-related activities can be very helpful for attention related problems and for general stress management for many ADD adults.

Question: Physical activity

a. Can help improve attention over the short term
b. Is helpful to channel energy and restlessness
c. Can lead to longer term hobbies and interests
d. Is a healthy and necessary part of life
e. All the above

Dr. Leon Schofield

Chapter 9: Self-talk, the Secret Weapon

The importance of self-talk

ADD children tend to have difficulty with what I call "self-talk", or internal language. Self-talk refers to the thoughts we have in our heads. This self-talk can be a few simple words, a short phrase or a long diatribe. Adults and children without ADD have more organized internal self-talk. We alert ourselves, repeat directions and questions, explore possible responses, problem-solve, and file information for later use. We plan and formulate an action or response. All of this occurs as a result of using internal language. Perhaps even more importantly, internal language helps us to modulate, or dim, intense reactive emotions. We literally talk ourselves down into a calmer place.

I have observed that hyperactive ADD children tend to have busy, chaotic internal language often jumping ahead, skipping important information presented to them orally or in writing. These children have self-talk that is focused on rushing to a conclusion and leaping into action. Their minds can also leap to unrelated subject matter. Emotions tend to be intense, raw, untamed by calming self-talk.

Inattentive ADD children are the opposite. They have little self-talk. Their minds will either be blank or it will be focused on some minor, unimportant feature not central to the topic at hand. Their minds often wander slowly away to irrelevant thoughts. Emotions may be more intense than they appear, however. When these children realize they are well off-task, they may be very anxious, though they may not show it. They often become withdrawn and avoidant, not disruptive.

If internal language or self-talk is lacking or if it is ineffective for ADD children, one way to improve their functioning is to help them to develop and manage their self-talk. Let's look at a few ways to help ADD children improve their self-talk.

Won't most ADD children see self-talk as stupid and useless?

They may. Parents need to remind them that this is not some weird, odd skill they need to learn. Self-talk is what most people do, most of the time. ADD children tend to either use self-talk to think about something off-track, or they use it minimally and ineffectively. Give them everyday examples of how you talk to yourself as you work through a problem, stay on track, or ease your frustration.

Step 1: Improve initial focusing with self-talk

The most obvious problem in ADD communication is what I call an "orienting problem." By this, I mean that the ADD child often is not even aware that someone is talking directly to them until the parent or teacher is several sentences into their communication. This presents obvious problems. What are the child's options when they tune in late? Option 1 is to simply state, "I wasn't listening; please start over." You know why they aren't likely to choose option 1. You will not be pleased to say the least. Therefore, they usually choose option 2, simply looking at you and nodding. This leads to other problems. Parents and teachers may walk away assuming the child gets it. You may ask them to "tell me what I just said." If they can't do that you may repeat your communication. Being really annoyed by now, you probably will just repeat it louder and faster. This will not help matters.

The solution to improving initial focus on the communication is to make sure that the receptive language channels are open. I would love to have your child say to himself, "OK. Let's pay attention here."

or "Okay, what's going on here." when you walk into the room or when a teacher stands up and walks over to them. This is not going to happen without some training. Have them practice stating such orienting phrases.

Parents and teachers should get an affirmative verbal response from the ADD child, in the form of a complete sentence, before proceeding. For example, your child may say, "Yes, I know you have something to say. Go ahead; I'm listening." Or they might say, "Okay, I'm listening; go ahead." A complete, logical sentence requires a lot more brain power than "okay" or a nod of the head. Bringing the language centers to the battlefield makes it more likely there will be success in the operation with a full battle force at the ready! The self-talk part comes into play as your child gradually learns to say alerting statements quietly to themselves.

Your child needs to learn to be alert to any changes in their visual fields too. Any movement, opening of doors, people getting up, should call your child's attention. Of course, auditory signals need to be addressed too. You need to be aware when someone speaks, or even when a door opens, or a chair is moved. You need to be ready to look and to listen when there are any changes in either the visual or auditory field around you. Have a discussion about this alertness issue with your child. They are often quite able to be alert, if they practice this and put it on a high priority. Have them practice this with self-alerting statements, "Okay, what's going on here?" or "Wake up brain; someone is coming in."

Acknowledge to your ADD child that it is difficult to pick up quickly on conversation and activity around them, but the skill can be worked on and improved. You can state, "For most people being aware and alert right away occurs pretty much automatically without much thought. ADD children and adults can do this but they have to coach themselves until they learn it."

Step 2: Improve processing of incoming information with self-talk

After we have paid attention to the initial communication, we have to process it. ADD children aren't great at this. Hyperactive ADD children have some brief initial focusing but soon leap off into other thoughts in their own minds. They have to work at staying on track. Often it's too much work and they will escape by daydreaming of something more pleasant. Their body is present, but not the mind. Here's where "self-talk" comes in.

We can have a discussion with our ADD child about what goes on in their head. Helpful self-talk is directing, positive and reinforcing. Examples include: "I can do this. Let's get going. Let's start here. Almost done. Good job." Unhelpful self-talk includes: "I hate this. I can't do that. I'll never finish. Bad job." You might remind your child that words have consequences as these words tend to direct their emotions and actions. Don't forget to explain again that positive self-talk promotes certain positive chemicals in our brain that help us to feel good and to stay on track. Negative self-talk produces negative chemicals that promote "fight or flight" to help us deal with what we believe is a threat.

Self-talk can go on to help with understanding and focus. For example, your child may repeat a phrase or sentence in their head. This captures the message of others and the replay gives your child a second chance to process it. Your child can also use self-talk to help clarify or question the incoming message. For example, your child may say: "I think I have to do ...." or "I don't understand ...." or "What was that time I was supposed to be back for lunch?" The standard approach of many ADD children is to just "delete" any messages that are poorly understood. Self-talk keeps your child in the game, and ready to process further incoming information.

Self-talk can be a bit funny; it doesn't help to be negative or self-attacking as we have discussed. Perhaps a child might say to himself or herself, "Okay brain, stop sleeping and wake up now!" Again, humor has its place.

Step 3: Improve sustained attention with self-talk

Self-talk can help sustain attention over a longer period of time. Sustained attention requires avoiding distractions, external and internal. The external distractions may be visual or auditory interruptions. Self-talk can help here by having your child stay on-task with re-focusing messages, a kind of self-coaching. Your child may say, "Okay, focus here." or "Back to work, brain!"

Fatigue is a big problem. ADD children need to work harder to stay on task. It literally is more tiring to attend over a longer period of time than it is for children without ADD. Again, self-talk statements can help. Your child may say, "I'm making progress." or "Half-way there." or "I can do this!" Self-talk may help them advocate for themselves too. Your child may say, "Okay, I'm tired and I need a break." or "My hand hurts from writing." This will allow them to move to appropriate management and self-advocating. They are more likely to seek relief before they reach a "blowup" or "I quit" point.

Step 4: Try virtual conversation

What will we remember better, a thirty-minute lecture, or a thirty-minute lively small group discussion? The latter, of course. The difference is in the participation. You are forced to really engage with others by focusing on their message, processing the information and formulating a response.

While anyone, child or adult, with or without ADD, is stuck in their seat listening to a lecture, or is stuck in a textbook reading some boring stuff, they are likely to drift off and absorb little, particularly if they have ADD. The solution is to have a virtual conversation or dialogue with the teacher or with the author of the book you are reading, in your mind. You need to interact "virtually" with the teacher or the author in order to maintain focus and understanding. Non-ADD children and adults do this a lot, naturally, without prompting. It is a natural coping mechanism. ADD children need to practice and prompt this.

I encourage ADD students to stop in their minds every few minutes and engage in virtual conversation or "self-talk" with the teacher or with the author. Virtual conversation can take the form of a summary: "OK, you mean...." It can take the form of a question: "I don't know what you mean by....." It can take the form of a criticism: "I don't agree with.... That sounds stupid." It can take the form of agreement or praise: "Wow, that's a great idea; you should get the Nobel Prize for that." The point of this is to engage the full brain at the highest language level for maximum focus and comprehension. Passive listening will work less effectively.

Reader Question: Does this takes the place of note-taking?

Note-taking is still important. You can write a short phrase or note on your tablet or in a notebook at a lecture. You can write a short phrase or note in the margin of your textbook, or in a separate notebook. Your brain will be even more engaged as you formulate the thought into a few written words. The key is "a few words." Don't expect to write a diatribe or an exact transcription of the lecture. If a critique or question is involved, you may actually refer to your notes near the end of the session when the teacher asks, "Are there any questions?" You have it written down, right there.

Reader Question: One more question. I don't think this method would work for me or maybe for my child. What if the dialogue in my head interferes with my listening? Wouldn't it pull some ADD children farther off track as they engage in "silly talk?"

Try it first before dismissing this. I find that many ADD children are going to "talk in their heads" anyway. This is just a way of directing and channeling the talk. With a little practice, they might get good at it. Sprinkle in a little exaggeration or sarcasm here and there, to make it interesting. Some ADD children may not be able to use this part of our self-talk tips. If it doesn't work, don't use it. Just do it the old fashioned way – sit up front, take or borrow notes, and try to prepare by pre-reading some lecture material or doing a quick scan of a text you are about to read to "get the brain ready."

Age appropriate collaboration

Various self-talk examples were offered above. Much of this is geared for younger children. Younger children will need more specific examples and modeling on your part. I would have them modify any of your suggestions to make it their own. Let them decide what they can say to themselves when they make a mistake, in order to minimize emotion and move on.

Older children can take charge more in considering what self-talk strategies might work for them. Though older children have better language capacity than younger children, they still might find internal self-talk to be a bit odd, a hard sell. Keep giving examples. Monitor your own internal thoughts and share them with your older child to model self-talk. Virtual conversations would be difficult for younger children to learn and use, but it's pretty natural for teens who are opinionated and confrontational anyway by their nature.

Let me offer one more thought here. Self-talk doesn't replace other organizational and reminder tips. It would still be important to have minimal distractions while you listen or read. It is still important to write down important information. It is still a good idea to write down your "to do list," and remember to take it with you.

Question: Self-talk is important because

    a. It helps your child repeat and reprocess incoming information.

    b. It helps your child consider coping strategies.

    c. It helps children with sustained attention as they drift or tire.

    d. It helps your child practice certain scripts to use in difficult situations.

    e. It helps when ADD children spot and reinforce their success .

    f. It helps because it can seem like you are having conversation with a teacher.

    g. All of the above

Chapter 10: Improve Communication and Social Skills

ADD and social skills

ADD children often demonstrate poor communication and poor social skills. They tend to act in an immature fashion, calling negative attention to themselves from adults and children. These ADD children often are seen as selfish, demanding and impatient. They are often seen as behaving inappropriately in a deliberate fashion. Parents often feel embarrassed by their child's poor behavior. Parents often feel they are being judged and blamed.

Part of the cause for this difficulty is a lack of effective practice. ADD children simply don't engage as often and as thoroughly as other children. Even when they attempt to socialize, ADD children also overlook important cues and rush through interactions due to their ADD. Another problem is that they have a tendency for greater reactive emotions, which create a greater risk of inappropriate behavior. High degree of emotionality tends to make ADD children "high maintenance" and less desirable as a friend.

In this chapter, we will look at the underlying deficits ADD children have due to their ADD which contribute to their commonly observed social skill problems. These issues include difficulty with:

- Picking up on cues and expectations
- Taking the perspective of others
- Staying on the social task
- Managing delays and changes in plans
- Handling frustrations and failure

Parents can help their child by coaching them to analyze and respond to the social demands around them. They can help their child use "social scripts" to manage difficult situations. They can help their child by practicing analyzing, problem solving and responding to social situations. Simply telling your child to "Stop it. Behave. Act your age!" will not be helpful.

Step 1: Help your child to read social cues better

The first problem ADD children have in this area is that they often don't look at the speaker. They miss many facial expressions and they miss the body language of the speaker. Much of what we "hear" when listening is actually visual in nature. So, the first step in improving communication is to actually look at the speaker.

The next part in this process is to use internal self-talk to focus and investigate. Children can "say" to themselves, "I wonder what this means?" or "How important is this?" Most ADD children can learn to identify what is expected and they can often identify the subtext; i.e., the emotion or effect associated with the message or task. The reason this is difficult may be that your child simply fails to even ask the questions. Most non-ADD children and adults automatically search for the details and underlying meaning of messages. ADD children must prompt themselves to do this. They still may need to ask for clarification. ADD children need to ask themselves, "What are they telling me here?" or "What is the time frame here?"

Your child may think they listen well and that they understand you or others. However, they need to accept that they are not always very accurate. Be empathetic. It's all part of the ADD. We all want to believe we are good listeners. However, because of the ADD, children need to take extra time to check often about the accuracy of their listening. Remind them that most people appreciate the extra effort your child may take to do this checking.

Step 2: Control the flow of information

ADD children and adults often have a problem with managing the flow of incoming information. They may think they understand or that they can keep up, but they often fall behind the speaker or they may become bored and jump ahead of the speaker to what they believe the question or task to be. I remind children they have to act like a traffic cop and stop or slow the information traffic down as needed.

Self-talk again will help here. Your child can say, "Stop! Whoa!" or "What is this all about?" The use of internal language helps your child identify the problem, reconsider the incoming information, and begin to formulate a coping strategy. They can rehearse in their minds a strategy to cope, such as "I need to stop here." or "I want to slow down." Internal self-talk helps your child begin to solve the puzzle of figuring out what the world is trying to say to our ADD children.

Of course, sometimes parents and teachers are guilty of speaking too fast, offering too much information, giving too long a "to do" list, or mumbling. Children can be encouraged to identify such problems and point them out to adults, politely. They can use a simple script, to use when they are lost or overwhelmed; i.e., "Excuse me, can you stop for a minute?" or "Can you slow down or say that again?" They can ask for clarification with a script, such as "Could you explain that again?"

A physical gesture is also part of communication. Even if the parent or teacher is communicating well, the ADD child's mind may wander, miss information, need clarification, etc. An ADD child might lean forward and raise their hand in a "stop" gesture before adding, "Could you please explain? Could you give me an example? Could you repeat?" etc. It is a good idea to also stop and check on your understanding, even if you think you know what's going on. Your child might say, "I think you want me to do.... Is that right?" Just pausing the flow briefly helps them repeat it in their minds and it helps to retain it better, particularly if repeated in written form. "Hold on; let me write that down."

Reader Question: Okay. I get it. But what about a child in middle school or high school, or even in college. If they have ADD, how can they control the flow of a teacher's lecture? Maybe you can ask one question, but you can't do much more about that flow of information. You can't stop the teacher every couple of minutes.

True. That's a different situation, I agree. Of course, you can tape-record lectures, or have a scribe take notes, or get a copy of a teacher's notes or a copy of a student's notes. Students can also have a "virtual conversation" as described earlier to help them maintain focus and sustain attention.

Step 3: Take perspective

It is hard for ADD children to get into the heads of other people. Partly this is due to their not looking or listening, which you would expect with ADD. However, the ADD problem is likely to be bigger than this. ADD children struggle with their own internal attention management. It takes ADD children longer to find information, hold onto several steps in a problem-solving sequence, find the proper word or phrase, identify and express their needs, etc. This internal struggle makes focusing on parents, teachers and peers even more difficult.

ADD children can take on the perspective of others and see things through others' eyes. But they once again have to remind themselves to do that. It's not automatic for ADD children. Again, internal self-talk can help. Your child can start this "taking perspective" process by asking themselves, "What is important here for this person?" or "What is their opinion?"

Reader Question: Aren't all children self-centered?

That's true. Developmental psychologists have long seen that it takes many years for children to see the situation from someone else's perspective. Simple judgments about right and wrong can be made by eight-year-olds. Deeper moral judgments don't occur until early adolescence. The ability to view events from another person's perspective occurs fairly early for non-ADD children. You can see this in the eight-year-old's negotiating skills. They know what you want and they will offer to meet it partly on your own terms and partly on theirs. Taking perspective, for many ADD children, is harder.

If ADD children are going to communicate successfully, they must ask questions, ask for clarification, and show an acknowledgement of their understanding. If unsure, they can question, "What do you want to do?" or "Tell me more." or "I don't think I understand."

Step 4: Stay on task

Working together on a social task or activity is a learned part of the social experience, but it is an area of weakness for ADD children. They may start out enthusiastic but they are likely to be bored or frustrated quickly. Many ADD children simply get up and walk away from a playmate who may be working on a puzzle or game. The ADD child needs to take a break, briefly. Then he needs to either return to the game or task or try to negotiate changing the activity. Interrupting an activity with a snack break works well. Adults can intervene in this way, but it is best to coach your child to try these tactics to help them leave the task or activity gracefully.

Preparation is often key. If some activities are planned for your child and friends, pre-activity discussions should occur between you and your child. There can be alternatives and back up plans as well as planning for breaks and "escape" if things go wrong. Part of the preparation should be anticipating what the friend likes to do and how to meet that need. ADD children can often figure out a solution or a path forward, but they just need a bit of time. They can "buy" time with these brief breaks. Just walking away to go to the bathroom or to go and get a snack can be a sufficient break. Adults do this all the time, buying time by getting a cup of coffee or checking on the kids or the dog. We all need to step away and restart our brains at times.

Reader Question: What if my child is clue-less. Shouldn't I step in to save the day?

You could do so. But that only teaches your child to rely on you or an adult to "save the day." You can take the child aside to "coach" him. Have your child think about what his friend does, what toys he has, what he talks about, etc., in order to give him some clues to the problem.

Step 5: Manage delays or changes

ADD children generally do not like delays or change. Yet, many social situations involve these elements. There often is a delay as you wait in line. There often is a change in plans, as you find the movie is sold out or the go-cart park is not open. The typical coping strategy is to take along something to do to cope with delays and change. An electronic game is the common tool used by most children, but a comic book or magazine will do. Have your child think about other options might work as a backup plan if plans are delayed or if they change.

A social script might be a good idea here, to help vent frustrations a bit as well as to help alert other children or adults to some distress issues. For example, saying, "I was really looking forward to this; that's a big bummer." or "I'm a 9 on my disappointment scale." can be helpful. It is important to communicate feelings as well as information. Most people understand and accept a measure of disappointment. But they don't want to see inappropriate behavior such as slamming a door, yelling about "unfairness," etc.

Step 6: Manage transition

A related problem for most ADD children is their difficulty in transitioning from one activity to the next. It makes sense that this would be hard for ADD children given the difficulty they have focusing. Once focused and on task, it is very tempting to move on. ADD children will often protest, "I'm almost done. Not yet. In a minute." They probably sense that if they are interrupted there is no returning. If they don't finish, they will not be able to get back to the point of their departure. They can seem rigid, inflexible and stubborn.

Once again, start with empathy, e.g., "I know it's hard to stop in the middle of something." If you have some further insights, you might add, "I know you worry that you will never get to do this." or "I know that you worry that the game won't be available at the store next weekend." Have a discussion about what might be done to ease the delay or transition. Have your child begin to problem-solve. Perhaps they can negotiate another time for the shopping trip. Perhaps they can order online. Perhaps they can distract their negative thoughts with another activity "to get your mind off this." Share such thoughts and activities you have used in similar circumstances.

Humor can work here as well. You might reflect how you obsessed over getting a particular task done, you stayed up half the night. It might have been a chore such as cleaning out the refrigerator. You felt forced, compelled to finish or something terrible would happen. "If I don't clean this all up, I'll never do it and there will be nasty mold on all the food and we will eat it and we will all get sick and it will be my fault." It might have been a game, such as getting to the final level. It might have been simply a fun activity, such as reading a book you can't put down. By sharing examples, you can laugh a bit at human behavior and apply these lessons to your child. This is more likely to be accepted by your child than scolding or lecturing.

You might share some self-talk you use when you need to transition or stop something. You can ask your child what self-talk they might use to lower stress, pull away, and go on to another activity. Maybe they can say things to themselves such as: "OK, I did really well; next time it'll be even better." or "You beat me, game, but I will get you next time." or simply "I'll get back to this later."

Of course, giving a warning helps too: "We leave in five minutes." But this may not be enough. There is often a surge in anxiety for these children as the clock ticks down and they still don't have a planned stopping point, or a way to capture their thoughts to that point, or a way to help with a return to task later. Having your child identify a good stopping point helps on several fronts. It helps them take ownership; after all, they picked the end point. It is a workable point in the time allowed; it's not overwhelming. It also helps them begin to formulate their thinking around partial completion of a task; letting go and stopping becomes less anxiety-provoking with practice.

Reader Question: Electronic games can be very addicting. Aren't ADD children even more at risk than other children for this type of problem? If so, maybe there is no "managing" for them. They just can't handle it. What do you think?

All parents struggle with this problem. I don't know if it's a bigger problem for ADD children, but it might be, given the issues of impulsiveness, problems with delaying gratification, and the high level of emotional reactivity. I have no problem having this discussion with your child. Point out that big blowups over a game is not acceptable and it is a sign that they can't manage playing without such incidents. Ask them to find a solution. If they can't come up with one, sanctions are okay. They can be limited to certain games, shorter time on the game, alternate days, weekends only, or none at all. Most importantly, ask your child to find a way to "stop and cool off" by either self-talk or distracting activities, or both.

Don't expect your child to come up with an immediate solution. Tell them that it will take time, and you can set an appointment time to resume the conversation. Of course, any sanctions you have imposed for the blowup remains in effect for now.

Step 7: Teach negotiation skills

ADD children don't negotiate well. Your ADD child may nag and beg. That's not negotiating. Most children learn to negotiate early in childhood. Non-ADD children are pretty good at "What if I do this later?" "I promise to do...." or "Can I get this done later after I have a snack?" Help your child learn to negotiate. Have them think about something they want to do or obtain, and how they can negotiate for it. Negotiation is a skill.

Negotiation needs to take into the account what the other party (you, for example) wants and why is important to them. Your child needs to first acknowledge the other party's needs and why they feel that way, before the other party will listen. Part of the solution they propose must take the other person's needs into account too, for a better outcome. For example, your child might learn to say things like: "I know you are worried that I might fail this class if I don't finish this book report … but I have a plan … can I talk about it?" This may lead to a more productive set of deadlines with specific responsibilities. Make sure the monitoring of this plan is also done mostly by your child. He or she can set up a set of goals, and a time for each and report back to you at specific intervals times.

Step 8: Manage frustration or failure

ADD children tend to blow up or walk away when they are frustrated or when they fail at a game or task. Pre-activity discussions can anticipate some of this and it can help your child formulate some alternative responses. Avoiding some games or activities that are high risk might be appropriate. Setting scheduled breaks is also helpful. Again, all of this should be done in collaborative discussions with your child.

ADD children can be very competitive, particularly hyperactive types of ADD children. You might suggest that your child could learn to ask their friend, sibling or even an adult to show them how to do something well or quickly. This early request for assistance helps your child moderate his or her own expectations. It also helps with bonding since most children and adults are likely to be happy and proud to demonstrate their skills. They feel good about your child too by association. Have your child actually role-play asking for help, speaking the words they might use to a friend, or to you.

Step 9: improve pragmatic language

Another area of limitation for many ADD children is a weakness in pragmatic language. Pragmatic language is the subtle meaning or expectation in a social situation. Good pragmatic language helps your child to understand what is expected and what is appropriate. Pragmatic language helps us identify cues offered by others that can help identify signal what should be done by us. ADD children often miss subtle cues, e.g., a gesture, body language or a slight rise in voice volume. They may wonder later why a parent is so angry! ADD children also often fail to identify what is expected in many situations. They may stand when others sit. They may talk loudly when others are whispering. They may get up when others wait to leave. They may not start a task when a parent or teacher signals by a gesture or word that it's time to start. They may not see the frustration and stress of others as they press your child to hurry a task along or get ready quickly. To others it appears that the ADD child is simply self-centered, or even disrespectful. The reality is that they often don't have the pragmatic language or verbal tools to cope.

For many ADD children this is an area of serious weakness. A simple reminder may not be enough. They may have to learn to "scan the room" as they enter to look for clues. They may be able to pick up what is expected right away. Part of the problem of missing social cues is that most ADD children don't bother to even look for them. They may have to ask in their heads, "What is going on here?" This again opens up some language areas of the brain and that script may nudge them towards greater recognition and understanding. If uncertain, they might use a script such as: "I don't know what I'm supposed to do now." or "Do you mean … ?"

Step 10: Consider counseling to learn social skills

Many ADD children need more than reminders and practice. They may need some professional counseling. Professional counselors have many techniques and suggestions to help your child. They have a large database to draw upon and their experience should be helpful. They also have the advantage of being "neutral" and not emotionally involved. Many schools offer individual or group counseling. The focus is generally on coping skills related to school work, but it also often spills over to social skill issues. Younger children may be offered a small group counseling program where they will learn to enter a group activity appropriately, to work on a game or task following basic rules, to wait their turn, to congratulate others, and to accept results – win or lose. The fact that the children in this counseling group are also struggling with social skills makes this a less threatening environment than in the general academic setting.

Private counseling is also an option. In individual sessions with a psychologist, your child may be able to identify the sources of the frustration and safely vent some of these frustrations. More importantly, your child can discuss and practice various social scripts and strategies to cope with frustration and failure. Parents should be involved too. They may have separate sessions to discuss strategies to teach and manage at home.

Reader Question: When should you seek counseling, either in school or outside?

That is a good question. I would certainly recommend this if there is any evidence of significant emotional or behavioral issues. Schools tend to focus on coping skills related to academic and social concerns in the school setting. Psychologists doing individual therapy outside of school tend to work on more personal and family matters, as well as general self-esteem issues. They also often communicate with your child's pediatrician, particularly if medication is involved.

Age appropriate collaboration

It is important for younger children to learn basic politeness. It is also important for them to begin to make an effort at reasoning what others might expect based on cues and setting, as well as based upon what is actually said by others. You can define this activity as a mystery. Like any good detective, they must seek clues and cues from the data around them. Parents can play that "game" by encouraging their child to imagine what strangers in a line might be saying to themselves or to others nearby. Your child might guess at what a parent might be thinking watching their child at a playground.

Parents can continue this educating process by reflecting on a recent event at home, repeating the words and tone they may have used. Again, what does this trigger in terms of your child's awareness of your emotional state as well as the information you are trying to convey? Let them struggle with it a bit, prompting a few possibilities if your child is truly stuck. However, make them work at it. Don't enable them and make them dependent as you explain what thoughts and emotions you or others might have in a certain situation. Challenge your child by offering a few possible responses your child may make and ask them to evaluate which would be better, and why. Help your younger child learn a few short, simple scripts to inquire about the situation. Practice these scripts.

Older children may be more sensitive to the thoughts and feelings of others. They have had some experience. The difficulty might be more in their struggle with how to respond to that knowledge. There are often immature responses, with a strong "fight" (argue or resist) or "flight" (avoid, pull away) due to a lack of skills. Older children have stronger language skills and might learn and practice some effective responses to a difficult social interaction, at home, in the neighborhood or at school. They can learn a bit longer and more complex "scripts."

Question: Communication skills are often immature in ADD children because:

- a. They fail to perceive or hear accurately what is going on around them.
- b. They drift in their attention and stop listening.
- c. They don't like delays or changes.
- d. They often react with excessive emotion, which blocks reasoning.
- e. They often don't negotiate well with others.
- f. All of the above

Chapter 11: Build Real Self-Esteem

Self-esteem deficits in ADD children

ADD children and adults struggle with low self-esteem. They live with the reality that at any moment they will face frustration and failure. ADD children tend to see themselves as defective. Somehow their frustration and failures must be due to their own lack of motivation, carelessness or lack of knowledge or skills that are typically possessed by everyone else. ADD children may act cocky and super-confident. But a setback or failure sets off all the old insecurities, even panic.

Self-esteem should not be confused with trophies, ribbons and certificates. In today's feel-good world, children start to expect rewards for just showing up. Grade inflation has made grades almost meaningless. ADD children are aware of this reality. They also discount the value of most awards and grades. Real self-esteem must come from their actual overcoming of real challenges.

One problem with raising self-esteem for children is that they have to wait for others to dispense the positive reinforcement. Those positive statements and recognition of good effort may take some time and, as we know, ADD children don't do well with delayed rewards.

Still another impediment to building self-esteem in ADD children is the difficulty they have in achieving at a high level of success in all areas – academic, athletic, artistic, etc. They may struggle with basic skills. They may lose interest quickly without immediate success. They may have a low tolerance of stress and frustration, reacting with strong negative emotions to minor failures.

They may simply tire with longer term efforts. All of this tends to push ADD children away from the basic hard work needed to achieve success.

In this chapter, we will explore several ways to help ADD children build real and lasting self-esteem. Higher self-esteem will keep them in the game, encouraging them to persevere.

Step 1: Identify strengths and skills

Children and adults, with or without ADD are usually more prone to think about their negative attributes than their positive ones. Remember, they are likely to get far more negative comments and punishment than non-ADD children. They might appear to be cocky and self-confident, but that is usually a "cover." In a quiet moment, try to have a discussion about what positive attributes and skills your child can identify within themselves. You can start the conversation by reminding them that most people, adults and children, are self-critical and often forget about their good points. Let them know that they don't have to demonstrate these positive traits 100% of the time. For example, they might be kind and caring for others, even if they fight with a sibling once in a while over a toy or game.

Some problematic behaviors may leak into the conversation. Keep in mind even some negative behaviors have a positive side. You can state, for example, that their high energy level can be a good thing; it helps not to tire out quickly. A certain stubbornness about a game or activity, might help them stick to a tough problem when they are adults. Their talkativeness and outgoing behavior, will help then meet and interact with many different people later. Of course, some of these traits can also cause problems. But they can be controlled "for the good" too.

Remind them that everyone messes up. It's natural. It's important to think about what went wrong and then to fix it, if possible. If it's not possible, it's important to think about a different way of dealing with a situation or problem in the future. Everyone struggles with being selfish or impatient. Everyone struggles with managing their emotions. We all strive to be better. They have a kind and concerned side too.

Having positive attributes and skills is money in the self-esteem bank. We all need to have a reserve of good feelings to see us through more difficult times ahead.

Step 2: Keep failure in perspective

We have already discussed the importance of anticipating difficulties and roadblocks. We have talked about developing strategies to manage frustration and failures. In order to help your ADD child to do the work of analyzing problems, developing coping strategies and learning to stay with tasks, they may need more than help managing a specific situation or task before them. They can benefit from a discussion about the general struggle in learning that everyone faces. Have a discussion with your child, pointing out that learning often leads to failures at first. That's how we all learn. Note too that all scientists try many things before their experiments work. The key is to not be afraid to try. When you do fail, the first step needs to be to study things and think about why it failed. What went wrong? Then you can think about how to fix it. Failure is not a problem. It is a normal part of learning.

You need to be empathetic with your child regarding their disappointment, but then encourage them to move on after a short mourning period. Move on quickly to "Okay, what did I learn from this and what can I do to fix this?" Set a brief time limit for sadness and self-recriminations. This allows your child to vent these natural negative feeling, but it then allows them to move on quickly.

Reader Question: Do you mean parents should set an actual time limit for dwelling on the negative? Shouldn't they take whatever time is needed? Maybe some children are more sensitive than others?

Yes, I mean an actual number of minutes, not hours or days. Of course, you may have an emotional "relapse" the next day because of a reminder of your problem or because of a similar setback. You can go back to the ten-minute grieving rule. You and your child should agree on a reasonable time to feel miserable. You should not be flip or silly about this. Be serious in stating your opinion that lengthy negative emotional displays set them back. Children and adults, with or without ADD, need to not wallow in misery. The sadness, fear, and hopelessness are all valid and should be acknowledged and expressed, but then it's time to move on to finding solutions. I understand that this may be difficult for your "sensitive children," as you have noted. But these are exactly the kids we need to strengthen or they can learn to live in a very negative world and expect little of themselves.

Step 3: Get off the beaten track

All children benefit from having some skill or interest that sets them apart, particularly if your child is struggling with success at school, sports and general social skills. As we discussed earlier, activities, mental and physical, can be beneficial. The benefits are not just improved attention, socialization and stress reduction. Development of a skill or interest improves self-esteem as well.

Looking beyond the obvious, mainstream activities has some benefits. There is some benefit in pursuing the more esoteric and unusual interests. There is less of an expected standard or path in these unusual interests and therefore less risk of clear failure. There is usually a smaller group of peers and few, if any, observers and therefore less performance pressure.

Help your child find interests that can become much bigger over time. A small interest such as building model planes, might lead to flying remote control planes, visiting warplane museums, trying a glider plane flight for teens, or visiting a school with an aeronautic program. Help your child find a passion and nurture it. Even artistic and creative interests can be pursued by most of us. ADD children often are happy to learn more about photography, guitar, jewelry making, cartooning, and writing.

The adult teachers and leaders will be very excited about their interests and will help your children reach that high level of enthusiasm and interest. Parents don't have to be "selling" the activity. Leave that to the adults who have a passion in what they do.

Step 4: Set the bar higher

Simple entry level activity will soon get boring. You and your child should aim high. After some dabbling in easy entry levels, start pushing the limits. If you are comfortable with a two-hour hike in a state park, consider an all day hike in a more remote location. Even the planning can be a self-esteem boost, let alone completing it. If you have learned the basics of chess, why not sign up for a tournament at the novice level? If you have mastered basic kayaking, then you might try a more extensive tour of a wilderness area. If you have tried a few exotic recipes, maybe you can sign up for a cooking workshop with your child. If you have an interest in history, maybe a trip to the local historical society would be interesting; be sure to strike up a conversation with the staff there.

As you begin to push the limits a bit, you will find the leaders, teachers and guides to be most informative, supportive and friendly. Your child will learn that learning is not always done at school and it can be fun. Self-esteem will flourish.

Step 5: Accept trying new activities

In terms of self-esteem, it may be best to be an expert at one thing. However, it is more achievable to be good at five things. Having varied interests has some benefits. First, having a few things to do can keep each activity fresh and entertaining. Second, the circle of people involved in that specific activity is likely to vary in personality, skills and interests as you move from activity to activity. Children interested in sailing are likely to be very different than children interested in art. Broader social contacts will allow your child to relate well with many different types of people later in life.

Of course, we don't want to encourage a series of quick looks at various hobbies and interests. Research it first and discuss what is involved in learning this skill, then agree to a reasonable time frame. What amount of time would be enough to learn basic skills? You can't decide on whether or not you have some talent doing something until you give it a fair trial.

Costs must be considered in any plans. You can't bankrupt the family or shortchange other children. It's okay to be realistic with your child about what is affordable. Your child can and should contribute to their interests too. They can do chores or use birthday money. Older children may have outside jobs for such a contribution. There is greater appreciation for what they have if they earn some of the cost. They may have to save up for that new kayak paddle or the cooking class. Waiting is okay for ADD children. Things can take time.

You can find many free or low cost activities in your community. Hiking is free. Many classes at your school, library or community center, or town's parks and recreation department are low cost. Check newspapers for activities in your area. If you are near any colleges, most will have a variety of lectures and demonstrations which may be of interest for older children. Most colleges are generally open to the public for a tour. I encourage older children from middle school on to visit a local college. Take a tour and learn what a huge and interesting world it is out there.

Age appropriate collaboration

Younger children might need a bit more direction from parents. You may want to research some activities available in your area. Begin by suggesting your child look at the positives and the negatives of a few activities. You will find this is better than asking them to say "Yes or No" to your offerings. Continue researching and gathering more information about the activities before making an opinion. This is excellent role modeling for the future. The automatic "No!" by your ADD child is likely to be triggered by lack of knowledge about the proposed activity or your child's fear that they will be incompetent. You can state this to your child. Thorough gathering of information can dispel fears. You can also join your child in the search for a new and challenging skill or interest for yourself. Find a challenge for yourself and talk about it often, noting the ups and the downs. Be a good role model.

Older children are likely to be a bit more independent and accepting of change, though that is not always true. Some older children are more inclined to see new skills and activities as enhancing their independence, helping them to be an individual and helping them separate successfully from the clutches of the family. However, some ADD children are dependent and fearful, avoiding any risks or problems they anticipate. This fearfulness and dependence is a major risk for future adjustment and success in all areas, educational, vocational and personal.

If your child is dependent and fearful, have a frank discussion with your child about the ways this limits their lives. Have a discussion about how they can wade into the pond slowly, trying a few activities that are comfortable at first. Then they can try more ambitious activities later. Set specific plans and goals. Don't settle for "I will try it someday." You might also consider counseling to help your child practice ways to overcome their dependence and fearfulness.

Question: Self-esteem is important since it helps us take risks and it helps us weather frustrations and failures. Self-esteem can be created by:

    a. Accumulating knowledge about a special area of interest
    b. Pursuing a skill that is out of the mainstream
    c. Setting the bar higher for some interest or hobby
    d. Trying several activities and hobbies
    e. Identifying strengths and skills
    f. All of the above

Chapter 12: Help Your Child to Manage Blowups

Poor reactive emotion management

We usually think of a child's blowup as a rebellious act, designed to control others. Blowups and meltdowns are actually primitive coping strategies, not usually rebellious and controlling behavior. They are signs that your child has no skills to manage the intense emotions they feel. Poor emotion regulation is common with ADD children. Many ADD children have very reactive emotional arousal. They see and feel setbacks and problems far more intensely than other children. Learning new skills to help this emotion-regulating process is essential to avoid serious problems and very bad outcomes for many ADD children.

Unfortunately, ADD children face an enormous amount of frustration and failure in their day-to-day life, at home and at school. As we noted earlier, they are often on the receiving end of negative comments or criticism at far higher rates than non-ADD children. This puts them at even higher risk for emotional meltdowns.

The coping strategies used by ADD children experiencing frustrating situations are generally rather primitive, i.e. "fight" or "flight." As we have noted earlier the fight side involves arguing, debating and verbally aggressive statements. With the more emotional, complex ADD children, this can escalate to throwing or breaking things or verbal and even physical fighting. The flight side involves shutting down, avoiding and procrastinating. This can escalate to depression-like withdrawal, self-deprecating comments (I hate myself. I'm stupid.) and behavioral stress symptoms such as nail biting, scratching, hair-pulling, and chewing on clothing or pencils.

Fight and flight strategies invite adults to intervene and control. It is understandable that parents feel they must intervene. While strong actions by adults may temporarily stop such negative behaviors, these actions don't help their child build better coping strategies. Helping your child to identify and manage their own emotions is essential.

Step 1: Understand the nature of the problem

Emotional outbursts of considerable frequency and intensity can be alarming. Are these emotional and behavioral problems true, separate emotional disorders or are they just ways to label the secondary effects of ADD for many children? Many of these children do improve greatly in their emotion and behavior management with modest, conventional ADD treatment. However, if the problems persist, these children are often given various diagnoses and labels. They may be labelled as "oppositional defiant disorder" due to their inability to conform to modest demands, and due to their explosive rejection of attempts to control and direct them. Older adolescents may develop behaviors leading to a "conduct disorder" diagnosis. They may act out their anger and frustration with inappropriate behavior. They may break rules at home, at school and in the community. Others may be given the diagnosis of "bipolar disorder" due to their rapid mood swings.

In my opinion and experience, the majority of these more serious diagnoses will diminish greatly or disappear when the ADD is under better control. Think about it for a minute. ADD is faulty functioning in the frontal lobes of the brain, the primary site for management and regulation of all our behaviors and actions. For many ADD children, faulty regulation extends beyond attention issues and into emotion management. Think of the frontal lobes of the brain as a kind of filtering system. It allows us to decide what we want to react to and to what degree it may be of importance. Another way to think of it would be to consider the frontal lobes of the brain as a kind of dimmer switch for emotions. If this system is deficient, we are likely to overreact to setbacks and problems.

A fairly small percentage of ADD children may also have independent emotional problems in addition to ADD. It is entirely possible to have a mental disorder in addition to ADD. ADD children are subject to the usual range of genetic problems including serious mental disorders, such as anxiety disorders, severe depression, bipolar disorder or autism. We must treat these separate problems, of course. In these cases, the attention problems may be largely secondary to the emotional disorder.

Reader Question: Okay, I accept that a child might be misdiagnosed as having a mental disorder, when the problems are largely due to ADD. Can the reverse be true? Can an emotional disorder produce the attention problem? And in a third scenario, a child might have both ADD and emotional problems as two separate problems. How can we separate these three possibilities if they look alike?

That's a great question. You have to start somewhere. You need to pick the most likely primary problem and treat it. Let's say the attention problems you are concerned about are pretty pervasive across a wide range of situations and settings. Let's also say that there is a family history of ADD either treated or strongly suspected. It makes sense to start your treatment with the ADD issues, even if there is a strong emotional component. If you get some improvement in attention areas, but emotional issues persist, then try addressing the emotional part.

Alternatively, let's say there is a strong family history of mental disorders, such as severe anxiety or depression. Let's also say that the attention problems in question are more situational, i.e., focused in one setting or around one activity, such as homework. Perhaps you would be best to start with a focus on managing the emotional problem first. If you get some improvement, but the attention problems persist, try addressing the attention problems then.

The need for counseling also increases greatly with more complex ADD cases, where ADD co-exists with emotional/behavioral problems. It is important for your ADD child to learn self-management strategies and not depend on others to do the work. Even medication has limits. Your child still needs to self-manage. Counseling can give your child some strategies to think about problems differently and to use better strategies to manage their problems.

Step 2: Show empathy

It is difficult to show empathy for a child that is pushing all of your buttons, but it is necessary. You can't sell anything without communicating understanding and empathy in the eyes of the buyer. You must try to get into the head of your child and relate what you see and feel in his or her shoes. The pressure, chaos around them and difficulty performing are huge obstacles. Reading books on the subject, including this one, can be helpful. You can find the language that may help you communicate with your child within these pages. Start out with a simple statement such as, "You must hate it when I ask you to clean up your room quickly." What child can resist that? You are an automatic ally by understanding their anger and frustration.

If possible, offer some examples of how you have practiced coping techniques in the past or more recently at work, avoiding a near meltdown of your own.

Reader Question: What if you don't agree with their point of view? What if you think you are making a simple demand, well within the ability to do it? How can I honestly be empathic then? I'm pretty angry at this point.

You need to step outside of yourself. This is not personal, against you. Your child feels overwhelmed and helpless, lashing out for self-defense. It doesn't have to be rational or accurate. You are not agreeing with anything. You are just listening and trying to understand their world. Hopefully you can help them tolerate and manage various demands at home and at school, but you won't be able to do that without this first empathic step.

You can admit to being perplexed and even concerned about your child's response, stating for example, "I know that you are upset, but I don't quite understand why at this point. Let's take a break and think about it before we talk." You can then go on to admit, "I don't really understand what is stressful for you now." You likely will need physical distance and time to cool off before you both can dig into the matter. You might offer possible options if your child is clueless about the cause of the blowup. "Is it this ... or is it ...?" Prime the pump, offer options and start the conversation.

If you can offer some personal history or experiences, do so. For example, "When my boss piled one more thing on my desk yesterday, I felt like blowing up and yelling at him to go away." Be sure you are being honest in your personal examples. Children know when you are exaggerating a difficulty or making it up. Be honest about the frustration, thoughts and actions, good or bad. If you are faking it or exaggerating the problem you're sharing, it will do no good.

Be careful not to ascribe your child's blowup to a big, permanent problem. Your child is not violent or crazy, though they may look and act that way briefly. They are also not permanently unable to do the task at hand. Consider that it might be just a bad time to do anything, and it may not even be related to the task. The blowup might have been on the heels of another problem on the bus or at school. Maybe the way you made a request triggered an outburst; you may have had a bit of an angry tone, speaking loudly and quickly. Perhaps there was a misunderstanding about the nature of the task and how fast it had to be done. Your child may be reacting to what they see as a big, impossible task in an impossibly short period of time. Keep probing and discussing, even taking notes, "so I won't forget anything." Of course, these discussions will take place after the emotions quiet down and not in the heat of the meltdown.

Reader Question: What if my child is throwing things or hitting? A simple timeout might not work.

Safety issues trump everything. If there is a concern that your child might hurt himself or others, you have to act. But just hitting the wall, or throwing a toy on the floor doesn't rise to that level. They can pick up, fix it or replace it later. I'm not suggesting they should not be responsible for their actions. Just don't allow your own emotions to drive you to an overreaction. If they need restraint, so be it, but don't be too quick to pull the trigger. You don't have to be happy, just neutral. For example, stating, "I know you're upset and stressed out right now, and I'm getting mad too, so let's take a break." Don't abandon your efforts to deescalate and reframe. Problem solving efforts must be postponed until emotional levels are lowered, on both sides.

Step 3: Defuse the situation by reducing stimulation and reframing

Parents and teachers often are perplexed, frustrated and even horrified by the explosions of these children. The child's behavior often leads to immediate emotional and behavioral responses that are supposed to manage this out of control child, but often have the opposite effect. Yelling, threatening, moving into their personal space, grabbing and holding them, etc., often produces greater emotional and behavioral problems. You might rationalize your own angry response as an attempt to control this child, or to defend yourself. But it is likely that your child has set off your own emotional overreaction. The child's reaction is not an attempt to "win" a battle for control, as many adults think. It is more likely a reaction to manage feeling overwhelmed and threatened. After all, even the smallest animal will fight if cornered.

The first order of business is to shut down the sensory experience as quickly as possible. You must remove the fuel for this fire. Look away, back away and reduce verbal comments to a minimum. Avoid lengthy lectures, comments, etc., and certainly avoid any verbal aggressiveness or threats on your part. "Stop right now! I won't be yelled at! How can you do that? Are you crazy? You are grounded for a month young man." This won't work. It's hard not to try to impose control and order, as well as to defend yourself. However, attacking at this point will only aggravate the situation.

You can reframe or label the outburst as "stress." You can label the feelings without attacking your child's motive or character You can also maintain a parental boundary without inflaming the situation. You might say, "You are really upset right now, and I need to think about that for a few minutes and you can too. We both need to cool off. I don't want to get into a yelling match here. We can talk later, not now." This defuses the situation immediately, leaves the door for discussion open, and indicates you will investigate the causes for this and that you expect your child to do so as well. It also begins the process of modeling more appropriate emotion management.

Step 4: Teach invisibility and "fighting withdrawal"

Your child will need to learn immediate coping skills in the goal to manage intense reactive emotion. We have discussed this a bit earlier, but these extreme outbursts require more intervention that promotes coping. I have had success with many children trying to reduce their emotionality by using two related techniques. The first is invisibility. When escape is not possible, such as in the classroom, your child can learn to look through or past the offending agent, teacher or child. Rather than blowing up and causing more problems, they can make the other party invisible and look through or past. Usually the teacher or child will run out of gas in a minute, unless your child provokes them with some type of verbal attack or some other inappropriate response. Breathe deeply and wait for the storm to pass. Show them how to do this and have them try it too.

Fighting withdrawal is another option. This is a military term. It is used to describe a situation where you must retreat in order to avoid a total defeat. However, you do so with some response. In the case of a child in an adverse situation, the response to an offending agent such as a child might be, "Okay, I'm not going to argue with you now and get into trouble." It might be even simpler, "Whatever." The response to a teacher may have to be more measured such as "Okay, I don't want to do this but I will try." or "Okay, this seems too hard, but I will try."

Without some verbal response to some interaction they feel is threatening or attacking, they will feel defeated and threatened. That will often lead to verbal and physical meltdown. I explain to children in this spot that most people understand that they can be upset. Expressing that emotion is okay as long as it is kept muted a bit, e.g., "I feel like I'm going to blow up, but I will try to sit down and get quiet." Others will often accept their emotion and they might even try to be helpful. But they will not tolerate oppositional behavior and verbal or physical outbursts.

Step 5: Explore underlying factors

You want to be aware of the big picture. Blowups often occur over minor things because the ADD child may have struggled over a long period of time, storing up stress, finally reaching a boiling point. Even adults get cranky after a hard, stressful day at work, blowing up later over a minor problem. Kids are no different. They often store up stress all day (like you may do at work), then let it out as soon as the bus arrives at home, or as soon as a simple request is made.

Parents can explain their concern about the big picture. Ask about your child's view of each part of the day, hitting even the little things such as lining up for the bus, the drive to school, getting to their locker, doing worksheets, going to lunch, etc. Collaboration should include the big picture. How would your child rate their level of stress at school or on the bus, or at home from 1 to 10. You might have to explain what would constitute a 2, 5, 8, or 10 level of stress. Furthermore, what outlets do they have to reduce stress and relax? You might want to explore ways you have relaxed, from childhood days to present. If you haven't had much relaxation in recent times, confess it and commit yourself to pursing more opportunities to relax. More on that in the next chapter.

Step 6: Make a plan to cope better in the future

In collaboration with your child, you need to make a plan that addresses the demands or tasks that tripped the meltdown trigger. Make a plan to avoid blowups and meltdowns in the future.

Again, try to have your child learn to recognize the signs and symptoms of their emotional arousal. This is important since many

ADD children aren't aware of the stress buildup and if they are, they don't know how to express it in words. It's hard for adults, with all of their language skills, to describe how and why they feel. They might identify their warning signs as increased loudness, scribbling their work, avoiding people, chewing on a pencil, etc. If you have seen some signs preceding blowups, you can share this as part of the discussion. It's important for your child to understand that blowups don't occur without cause and without warning. Again, consider using a number rating system with the caution that it should be an accurate measure; not every problem is an automatic 10.

Another point of collaboration is to discuss a safe place for your child to withdraw to in order to cool off. This might be their room, the garage, the basement, a tree house or at school, perhaps the nurse's office, the psychologist's office, or a quiet corner of the classroom. Getting into a quiet, relatively isolated place helps with the unwinding process.

Your child needs to learn to apologize; many ADD children struggle with this simple action. They need to say, "I'm sorry I yelled at you. I was in a bad mood from school." They need to hear from you, their coach, that an apology heals wounds and makes allies. Say it using those words, then explain what you mean by wounds (hurts) and allies (support). Don't talk down to your children. Elevate them, giving them new language and new skills for self-expression.

Restitution relieves guilt and raises self-esteem. They can learn to fix things, by cleaning up or by helping the parent, teacher or another child. Sometimes restitution can't be made directly since the problems were words and actions, not physical damages. Offering to help the other party after "I'm sorry about.... Can I help you out?" can be extremely helpful. Describe how you feel on the receiving end of such apologies and offers of restitution. This is not rocket science.

These are things kids learn to do and your ADD child can learn this as well. It just has to be modelled and practiced a bit more before becoming automatic.

Step 7: Consider expanding medication management

There are a wide range of additional medication options beyond the usual stimulant medications. For example, there can be substantial reduction in anxiety with certain antidepressants such as Prozac or Zoloft that have stress reducing benefits. Antihypertensive medications can also be helpful to some degree. These medications are often combined with stimulant medications. You can discuss medications with your child's doctor. Your doctor may also want you to consult with a pediatric psychiatrist or pediatric neurologist regarding additional medications if they don't feel comfortable using medication other than the stimulants.

Step 8: Consider counseling

Counseling for your child can be very helpful. Be sure to find a counselor experienced in the treatment of ADD. Many counselors, psychologists and social workers see children with ADD but it is not their specialty. Ask your child's doctor, school staff and parents of ADD children who they recommend. Don't be hesitant to interview the perspective counselor. Present your problems clearly and ask them what strategy or approach they would use. Be sure to ask if they also offer strategies for parents to use at home. Ask them if they offer frequent feedback. Ask them if you can call if you have questions. You might have to pay for a private consultation to discuss this in depth, but it is worth it. Remember you are starting what might be a long-term treatment plan.

If counseling seems to be taking shape as a part of the treatment plan, have a talk with your child. Listen to their concerns without judgment. Ask them to clarify and explain their likely initially negative reaction. Explain that you also have reservations. Discuss what you have done as part of your research. This conversation is a teaching tool to help your child identify and select helpers in the future. Tell your child you understand and empathize with starting something new. Point out the advantages of being able to say whatever is on your mind to someone who will listen and provide support and recommendations, without judgment. Finally, agree on a reasonable time period to review things. It might be appropriate to take a "vacation" from counseling for a few months to try some techniques they have learned. It might be appropriate to end it if it's not helpful.

Step 9: Adjust educational planning

The educational planning is likely to be more complicated for children with complex ADD, since the ADD is only part of the picture. There will be emotional and behavioral problems to address along with significant academic skills weaknesses. Usually an IEP will be necessary in these cases. Services at school will likely be needed, such as reading, occupational therapy and counseling. Many children also require a smaller classroom setting with an aid in the room along with the teacher, who is likely to be a special education specialist.

It may sound like these children are bound for a limited educational and vocational experience. However, in the proper setting with sufficient support, many of these children will move on to college level and self-sufficient lives. Nature has a way of working around problems and many of these children will develop good coping strategies and they will find their niche in life. In psychological research over the years we have learned that most changes for children occur abruptly after some development of minor coping skills, and finally after practicing alternatives. Sometimes after a long struggle with minor gains, there can be a major shift in improved coping abilities. Look at progress as a stairway, maybe with a few landings along the way, not a single upward straight line.

Reader Question: One final question. What if my child has developed a habit of blowing up in order to get out of doing something? Is that a possibility?

Yes, in fact it's likely if this is a long-term problem. It just may be a habit or a kind of coping strategy, albeit not a very good one. Yes, it is manipulative in a sense, but that doesn't negate the child's discomfort and lack of confidence in his capacity to deal with the issue at hand. It's just one more problem to address, in addition to the poor coping skill issue.

You can have a calmer discussion later about noticing the patterns here. Then discuss why this way of coping, this habit, produces more problems. Most children will be able to see how that works. They also probably would agree they would like to cope better, but they don't have the skills. Empathize with this dilemma and commit to searching for better ways to tackle big stress situations. Counseling again may help here, but on the spot reflection, planning and practice is still going to be needed, with or without counseling. Don't expect a counselor to find a miracle cure, especially one where you have to do little or no work.

For example, let's say your child has blowups over homework. He may be struggling with writing tasks. After some research (looking at the work, talking with the teacher, having some discussions with your child), you may conclude, along with your child, that the problem is largely due to the difficulty of getting thoughts onto paper. The struggle with the writing may be partly the physical act of writing and partly the writing skills themselves (spelling, grammar, punctuation). Your child might do better if you have him or her dictate thoughts which you can type. You likely will find your child has very good understanding and very good ideas about a topic. Point that out! Your child can read and edit your first typed effort. You can also ease your child into the editing role by asking them to give you an alternative to the sentence you just read. Later they will be able to do their own editing, hopefully.

Beyond the writing difficulty your child may see this performance issue as a death sentence academically. If he can't do these basic assignments, his academic life and future are doomed, in his eyes. No wonder he's angry! You can move beyond the immediate problem and discuss how many bright and successful people are not good at writing. Your child might laugh at the idea of having a secretary or typist write for them when they are a CEO or a doctor. Point out that such a situation is not crazy. It happens all the time. In fact, it is probably better to hire someone to do this and put your talents mostly into doing the big things like creating a company or providing a new hip for a patient. Which is better, doing the important work or typing memos and notes?

Point out to your child that other people, including even you, sometimes don't understand why something might be difficult for them. Remind your child that the teacher, and even you, can't get into your child's head. Remind your child that they don't always understand what might be the problem. Tell your child that they will need to learn an appropriate way to communicate when they need help. That process of learning about yourself starts with letting people know the level of your distress at the moment, maybe by using a short phrase (I'm really stressed out) or even a number. (I'm at an 8 out of 10!)

Teachers are often likely to try to be helpful. They don't want a big scene and more problems and they are likely to be genuinely empathetic. If the teacher is in a "bad mood," however, tell your child that they must take a breath and say, "I'll try, but it is hard." Teachers aren't always patient and helpful. I'm sure your child will agree with that! But it is important to give your teacher a chance to be helpful. Most of the time it will work out well. Maybe the problem is not so clear cut. If your child doesn't know why they are upset, it's okay to say that too. Think about it though; don't accept "I don't know," without some contemplation and effort on their part.

Before leaving this topic, I want to again emphasize that there are many ways to get to a goal line of relative success, academically, vocationally and socially. The answer is a mix of learned new skills and accommodations in both the goals and the path to those goals. Be flexible. Be watchful. Your child will often give you hints about what are reasonable goals, and how to proceed to those goals. We may slow that progress inadvertently by thinking in terms of conventional goals and conventional paths to them. Think outside of the usual parental box. For example, your child may do well with a small social group, a small classroom setting, unusual hobbies or interests, individual sports and physical activities, a slower academic pace, an extra year in college, a job suiting his skills and interests, etc.

Reader Question: Can you live with us for a few weeks?

Thanks for the invitation. However, I am tied up at the moment. I understand it is easier to teach and plan, and much harder to do. Remind your child that this parenting thing is not so easy. You have to learn parenting by some trial and error. You don't have to be a PhD psychologist here, just a concerned and loving parent who is trying.

Age appropriate collaboration

You are probably wondering how an ADD child with both attention and emotion management problems can be able to collaborate in the diagnosis and treatment of their ADD? Collaboration is particularly important here, since this type of child is very likely to slip into serious helplessness and dependence and that can result in a very serious long-term problems, emotional and behavioral. Complex ADD children need to know, understand and proactively manage their own limitations.

Suggestions are offered above to help your child identify and manage intense emotional reactions. We are used to seeing this problem more obvious in younger children who have problems with judging and controlling their behaviors on a good day, even without ADD. Younger children simply have less experience and training than older children in this area.

Younger children need to deal with more immediate frustrations and failures. They don't have much of a longer term vision. They need more discussion, modeling and practice managing difficult situations. Be sure to notice and praise even modest changes in your child's verbal and physical actions that suggest they are trying to learn new coping strategies. If you see some small behavior that might help with emotion management, such as looking down briefly or asking, "What do you mean?" offer your praise. The small steps made now will build big changes in the long run. Tell them that too. Create a positive long-term vision for your child. Spotting progress for them whenever you see it reinforces you as well. It helps you to avoid being discouraged.

Older children may not have the big meltdowns, but they may be prone to angry outbursts, avoidance and passive aggressive behavior. This can be exasperating for parents. Look at such behavior as their primitive attempt to control their own fears and frustrations. Older children may be driven to extremes too because they do actually see their future, and it isn't pretty, to them.

Both younger and older children need to learn to recognize and manage their emotional reactivity. They need to channel their excessive emotions into more constructive paths. With the empathy and support of parents, as well as with counseling support, they can learn to manage these emotions more effectively.

Question: Complex ADD children with significant emotion management problems in addition to ADD problems:

a. Have strong reactive emotions, with less ability to modulate or reduce these emotions
b. Have much less tolerance for situational stress that most children cope with
c. Need more complicated treatment, both medication and counseling
d. Likely will need a more comprehensive educational plan with varied accommodations
e. Still need to work on coping skills and self-management, like all ADD children
f. All of the above

Dr. Leon Schofield

Chapter 13: Parents, Take Care of Yourself

Who takes care of the Parents?

We often neglect to take care of ourselves, in the service of others, particularly when it comes to our children. Caring for an ADD child can be exhausting. The parent of an ADD child often may face a different kind of challenge than parents with children having a physical handicap. There are no wheelchairs or crutches with ADD children. The ADD child has no outward signs of disability. Their inappropriate words and actions appear to be voluntary and intentional. Others often assume the parents are to blame for their child's poor behavior. Others may conclude that there is inadequate training and supervision going on at home. Even extended family may be critical of your parenting.

I want to emphasize the strain on marriages which often occurs with ADD children, particularly if their child is overly emotional and he or she is prone to aggressive and disruptive behavior at home and at school. Parents can figuratively and literally split over disagreements about the management of their child. I have often found that parents with very divergent opinions can both have a good point. Unfortunately, divergent opinions often push parents apart.

Any child will notice this gulf between parents around management differences. They may exploit this difference in order to achieve some short-term gain. In the long-run though, the ADD child is well aware that they are at the center of the dispute and they are in many ways responsible for the strain in the parents' relationship. If separation or divorce occurs, they likely will feel like they have caused this, even though the ultimate responsibility lies with their parents.

Step 1: Avoid overload

It's easy for parents to get overly committed. They often have to add time for counseling, tutoring, homework, after school clubs, play dates, and doctor's visits in addition to an already busy family life. The amount of supervision needed at home to manage an ADD child is also much greater than for non-ADD children. Signs of overload for adults include: irritability and overreacting to minor setbacks, forgetfulness and minor mistakes, avoiding or resisting activities that used to be fun, fatigue and slowness doing basic tasks, undone chores and basic maintenance problems in terms of putting things away, organizing, etc., and the absence of meals together, or half your meals eaten at fast food places.

If you feel overloaded and overwhelmed, you are overloaded and overwhelmed. Look around you. Consider what you do for your children, spouse and family as a whole. Perhaps it's time to delegate some of these chores, eliminate others and ask your ADD child to step up as well. Perhaps some of the child-centered activities are not needed; the gains may be minimal and not worth the stress on yourself and the family. Make a commitment to have twenty minutes a day at least of "alone time," focusing on your personal interests. Discuss this with your family. They may agree that many activities have minimal value and can be eliminated.

Step 2: Nurture and respect your marriage

Your spouse is not your enemy. That may not be so obvious when you are at odds. Like any good negotiation, you can only heal by listening. Commit yourself to listen and not judge. It is very possible that your spouse may have a good point. You can state that you disagree, but you still need to ask questions, ask for clarification and examples, and ask for details regarding their child management strategy. Ask your spouse to listen to you as well, with the same inquiring mind-set. Ask your spouse to share the range of feelings they have at this time. Just listen. Then take a timeout, offering no immediate feedback or critique. Agree only to give each other's opinions and thoughts a close look. Agree only to continue the discussion later, at a specific time, for further sharing. Postponing any negotiations will allow both parties to lower the emotionality. It will allow both parties to be more receptive and understanding of one another.

Try to look at any changes in parent management approaches as experimental. Have an agreed-upon fair trial. Agree to jointly discuss this new approach with your child. Agree to listen and consider any modifications your child may suggest. But present a united front in the end.

Step 3: Share duties

Often one parent seems to take on the vast majority of the burdens. Usually it is Mom, but that can vary in today's world. Consider first that all parents bring certain skills to the table. Excluding one parent may miss his or her valuable contributions. Also, having one parent in the marriage be in charge of raising the ADD child is a sure-fire recipe for failure, through exhaustion as well as through the likely conflicts that will be generated between parents.

Make an assessment of skills and interests that both parents have. Make an assessment of how much time each parent may be able to devote. Make an honest assessment of what drives you crazy about your ADD child. One parent may prefer to assist with bedtime, another with homework. One may prefer to read to your child; another may prefer physical activity. One parent may prefer to organize and write certain concerns for teachers and staff at school. Another may prefer to talk face to face with the teacher. One may prefer to take the lead at the next school meeting. The other may prefer to take notes and perhaps address a specific area of concern. Take time to talk it out and agree to share the burden and responsibilities.

Step 4: Have a quiet zone

It's nice to plan for a weekend break to shop or have coffee with friends. But the stress does not wait until the weekend. Stress is now, not next Saturday. You need a break now, not next Saturday. It's helpful to have a scheduled "timeout" or break when you can walk, read, listen to music, etc. It takes at least fifteen minutes to get rid of nasty stress chemicals in our brain. Another fifteen minutes might bring true relaxation and restoration.

Reader Question: Hold on. We have a crazy schedule. The only "free time" I have is at 11 PM when everyone is in bed. Then I usually use my "free time" to clean up. Fifteen minutes sounds impossible during the day or early evening.

Listen to yourself. You've gotten into some bad habits. You sound like a prisoner in your own home or some kind of martyr. Who's in charge here? Take action and make it happen. It's not unreasonable to have twenty minute breaks for yourself. Your child is not in intensive care. At the appointed time your child can retreat to their room and busy themselves with some activity. They can play a game, read, build. Any disturbance in your rightful request will be met with sanctions.

Step 5: Parents, develop a hobby or interest

You are more than a parent. You are a human being with skills and interests beyond parenting. Make sure you don't abandon yourself. If you do abandon your interests, you will eventually feel tired and resentful. It's important for you to make time for your hobby or interest outside of the home. Why not bring that hobby or interest front and center into the home? Hang up your painting or wall hanging. Find a fancy pot for the orchid you are growing. Display your books about history in a prominent spot at home. Hang a picture or poster or your favorite singer, writer or sports star. Be a good example. Life is more than school or work.

Don't give up on this hobby issue, even if time is limited. You may not have the time to play eighteen holes of golf every Saturday, but you can hang a poster, read a golf book and talk about your best shot ever at dinner. You may be able to get away for nine holes of golf once a month. Maybe you can even ask your spouse and children for advice. What do they think you should try? It might be surprising to hear what your family might suggest. It could lead to a lively discussion. You can turn it around and ask your children what they would do for a hobby when they are an adult.

Step 6: Care for your physical needs

It goes without saying – a healthy life requires a good diet, sleep and exercise. It's hard to achieve these reasonable goals in today's world, with or without an ADD child. Most likely the whole family is in need of an examination of these needs. It would be a good idea to ask everyone in the family to contribute their opinion about what constitutes a healthy life.

Make a personal and public commitment to improving your life. Discuss and ask for suggestions regarding each of these health areas, i.e., diet, sleep and exercise. Search for some healthy snacks and desserts. Reduce the use of unhealthy food or drink. Get enough sleep. Announce and track your progress. Pick a single, specific exercise you plan to do within or outside the home on a daily basis. Again, discuss and track this openly. Plan some outdoor, active activity that will include all the family. Make it an adventure. Be a good example and the troops will follow – with a little prodding.

Dr. Leon Schofield

Step 7: Appreciate and value yourself

It's easy to see what you've done wrong or what you have failed to do. But it's important to stop and give yourself credit for the effort at least, even if you fall short of your goal. Share your success and partial success with your family. They need to hear good news sometimes. You need to hear yourself talking about the good news. Be a good role model in this regard.

Encourage others in the family to identify their strengths or skills. Have each person identify a strength or skill they see in others. Sometimes it's difficult to appreciate this in yourself. Even the ADD child has skills and strengths. Discuss this and consider that such positives don't have to lead to awards or public recognition. Being kind to animals, wanting to learn how things work, having the guts to try something new, overcoming a fear, won't get you any prize money. But you can be happy to have these skills or traits.

Step 8: Attend or create a support group

Finding support networks can be difficult for parents. The advantage of supportive listeners is that they can provide empathy, patience and helpful suggestions. Ask your child's pediatrician or your child's school psychologist if there may be an ADD parent support group in your area. Check ADD chat rooms on line to see if you can find the right support there. Find a friend, neighbor or relative who does listen well without harsh judgment.

Special Challenges to Taking Care of Yourself:

Many of you are or will become single parents. This will present an even greater need to care for yourself. You probably will try valiantly to be both parents. You can't go it alone. Seek the support of other relatives and friends. You need the objective advice.

Sometimes you just need a shoulder to lean on and someone to just listen. You need to rely on others to provide brief child care, transportation, tutoring and leisure activities. Offer to help out other parents too. They can use a break, even if they don't have ADD children. Don't neglect yourself. It's not selfish to take good care of yourself. You can't take care of your child if you haven't taken care of yourself.

Another special challenge involves managing an ADD child who has serious emotional and behavioral problems. This book does not address these difficult situations. While some of the suggestions offered here will be helpful, these troubled children will need far more resources than you can provide. Talk to professionals in your area to learn about services for your child. These children may be eligible for day treatment services, special summer programs, at home counseling, special needs programs and respite care. Ask professionals about counseling for yourself. It is important to be able to talk about serious matters freely and openly with a neutral party in confidence. Some things you can't say to your friends and family.

Age appropriate collaboration

Your ADD child's helpfulness in terms of pointing out their parent's strengths and skills is a kind of collaboration. Your child can begin to see that the world does not revolve around them. Parents have needs too. Your child can see some value and even personal gain in guiding or supporting you. Your child can see some value and personal gain in their making a small sacrifice in their own needs and interests to serve and support others, especially you.

If your younger child suggests you take up sky diving for a hobby, you can have a chuckle but pass. Then you can point out the merits of the general part of the suggestion. Maybe it would be a good idea for you to try something a bit exciting and even risky, with some help and training of course. It might involve hiking, sailing or public speaking – not sky diving. Older children may offer more appropriate suggestions. Maybe these older children can begin to think about their own parenting skills they will need for their children in the future.

Question: Parents, taking better care of yourself:

    a. Improves your self esteem
    b. Provides a necessary recharge for you
    c. Is a good role model for your ADD child
    d. Helps reduce burnout
    e. All of the above

Chapter 14: Prepare Your Child for the Future

They do grow up

I do not have a crystal ball that will tell us how our ADD children will fare as adults. Much of what our future holds is often determined by chance events and by the corrective measures taken. The opportunities and the challenges anyone faces tend to set us on very different paths.

When we consider ADD, it is important to know that there are many successful and happy ADD adults out there. Some may not even be aware they have ADD. These "hidden" ADD adults may have been lucky. They may have had good support at home and at school. They may have a strong motivation to achieve and good emotional resiliency. Some of that drive and resiliency may be genetically based; they may have an abundance of positive brain chemicals that help a great deal.

On the other hand, if there is little or no treatment of ADD, there is often a far greater chance of a negative outcome. These negative outcomes have been explored and appear to include less education, lower job status, less income, more job changes and more moves than peers with similar intelligence and similar socioeconomic background. There is also greater risk of anxiety and depression in untreated adults with ADD, as well as greater risk of alcoholism and drug abuse.

Let's examine some steps you can take to tilt the balance towards a positive outcome as your ADD child enters adolescence and moves into young adult years.

Step 1: Work on improving education

Education is generally the secret to success. Educational support starts with early elementary grades, as we have seen in this book. Early identification of ADD and providing appropriate accommodations are helpful in reducing future risk. Tutoring and summer programs focusing on building basic reading, writing and math skills are crucial. Private tutoring during the year can be helpful as well. It can take the pressure off of your relationship with your child. It can help them learn to seek help from others outside of the family.

Education doesn't end with high school. If traditional college is desired, you can evaluate issues like the size of the school, the course offerings, the counseling services, and the extent of services provided by the students with disability office. The name for this type of service varies from school to school. There is a wide range of criteria for receiving accommodations in various colleges. Some colleges are more relaxed in their acceptance of ADD accommodations, while other colleges may be very strict and provide few, if any, accommodations. They may require that the ADD child must have severe deficits before services can be offered. The services also vary widely for students with ADD or LD (learning disabilities). Be sure to look at the college's literature carefully and make some calls. Some parents send along ADD testing data and request an early review by their child's perspective college's students with disability office; they should be able to give you some idea of what service the school will provide for students with a similar profile, even before you have formally applied.

Another approach to college might be to take a class or two locally and work part-time. This will allow the ADD student to dip their toes in the water. They can get used to a college pace, which is fairly accelerated. They can get used to working independently, unlike high school which is more closely supervised with daily homework, numerous quizzes, papers, etc. Some students prefer online classes because of the flexibility and freedom they have in "going to class."

There are many other options besides traditional college, if that is not a good fit. There are many technology-oriented careers at community colleges. Many ADD students prefer to have a shorter pathway to a job. The long-term liberal arts approach may not be a fit for all. Another alternative is long distance, online programs. If it's too quick, too easy and too cheap to be true, you may want to take a pass.

Always leave options open. Taking a break from school for a year or two is often a good idea. Many employers offer incentives for their employees to continue their education. Work can also help the ADD young adult learn about their strengths and interests.

Step 2: Develop after school hobbies and interests

Education occurs outside of the classroom too. Your child may benefit from taking workshops and summer camps in areas of interest such as sailing, camping, robotics, art, creative writing, and computer technology. The skills learned help improve self-esteem and social skills by virtue of interacting with a wide range of educators and students from varied backgrounds. Learning new skills also improves resiliency or the ability to manage a complication or roadblock without depending on parents.

Having a special skill or talent has been shown to have a positive effect on adult success later in life. Being an expert in some area is really beneficial. I have seen many ADD children happily talk about their subject of interest. One such child recently noted proudly that she is a "shark fanatic." She did know a lot about sharks! The self-esteem bank gets some deposits as their special skill is shown or discussed. There will be challenges ahead that will require some withdrawals from that account so you can't get enough self-esteem points in the bank.

Step 3: Surround yourself with positive family and peers

This sounds like a simple idea, but how often do we think about who we are in daily contact with? We may tend to gravitate towards others who are pretty lazy or even angry about their lot in life. If we hear negative messages all the time, we will quickly learn to mimic these attitudes and set the bar quite low. Worse still, we may take a path that can be destructive. Negativity also sets off negative chemical reactions in our brain as we prepare for problems, allowing the downward spiral to continue.

Parents can encourage their ADD child to have contact with children who have a positive outlook. They can encourage contact with children who have positive values, interests, and activities. There may be a cousin or uncle or aunt out there that is positive and supportive of your child. Encourage time together.

Step 4: Help your child chose a realistic and viable future path

This is a bit tricky. ADD children and teens tend to be a bit immature. This can mean they may develop goals that are unrealistic. They may want to be a veterinarian but they lack the academic skills for that. They may want to be a star basketball player, but they don't have the physical build or skills needed to make it. They may want to be a rock musician, but they are only fair at their instrument. Parents can be caught in this dilemma. Should they discourage the fantasies?

I would certainly praise a child's interests and encourage them to learn more about it. I would encourage them to work on their skills. However, I would remind them that work opportunities are often difficult to get. They must have a "day job." They should be looking at educational and vocational paths that have some similarity to their interests. They can and should continue their interests as a hobby or sideline. Offer the example of many local people who play in a band or try community-theater. They do this as a hobby, not as their main employment.

Reader Question: I get it. But if your child has an interest that has some limited possibilities, what can you do? My child wants to be a writer. There's not much chance you can make a living writing fiction.

That is a good example. As a parent-coach, you can begin to inquire; what types of jobs do writers get? Together you might investigate the Occupational Outlook Handbook and other career resources material. You will soon get a realistic picture from an objective outside source. You don't have to be the villain. Most of these resources will give you alternative options which may have a career path. Perhaps a major in communication will work, leading to journalism or marketing. Writing skills may be very helpful for other fields too. You can encourage your child to continue to pursue fiction writing, but they might step it up a bit by taking a creative writing class at school or in your community. Perhaps they can submit their writing to a children's writing competition or they can submit their work to a children's magazine. The important part is to get out there – get feedback and critiques. Don't just sit in your room and wait for the Nobel Prize in Literature.

Keep in mind too that the majority of college students change their major at least once in their journey to the Bachelor's degree. Encourage your child to explore courses in a wide range for the first two years if they are unsure about a future goal. You may surprise yourself and find something you were not looking for. I know, I changed my major three times in college. When I found psychology, it felt like a good fit. However, I still had to try several psychology classes before deciding what I wanted to do within that field.

Step 5: Plan exercise and routine

It is easy to get into a more sedentary life as a young adult. There is no PE class or sports team for most young adults. Many ADD adolescents have been quite active in sports at school or at their local Y." As they move on to young adult years, that regular exercise and tight scheduling is suddenly gone. The structure and discipline of sports helps with completing tasks, in addition to the direct attention boost that that comes with aerobic exercise, as we noted in chapter 8. Fortunately there are usually excellent fitness center facilities at most colleges along with running tracks, pools, tennis courts, etc. Your child can consider a club sport, instead of a varsity sport. It will have far less time demands. He might learn a new sport and find friends to join in. Encourage daily physical activity of some sort. There are many adult exercise and sport programs available in most communities if they are not in college.

Another big problem with college is the variable schedule from day to day. Their school day is likely to be packed some days, and it may have just one class on another day. They may start their day at 8 AM or at noon. They also have about a third of the time in class that they would spend in high school classes. The other two-thirds of their day should be devoted to studying independently, of course.

All of this "free time" needs to have some structure. ADD college students need to create a study schedule and a place to study, and follow it. They need to establish a "mini goal" for each period of study, as we discussed earlier. Just "studying for a while" is way too general and will likely accomplish little. The ADD college student needs to be up at the same time each day, though their schedules and activities may vary wildly from day to day.

Discuss with your child your concerns that the academic semester is generally about fifteen weeks compared with the high school semester of about twenty weeks. Most colleges expect more work, in both quantity and quality, in a shorter time. So how will your student plan to cope with that? This should be discussed first, not discovered later.

Part of the routine may include assistance at the school learning center. There is often abundant help available. Many schools have extended hours and help available in a wide range of subjects. They often offer help with study skills, preparing for papers and projects, etc., in addition to formal accommodations, such as extended testing time in a quiet area. Incidentally most colleges that grant testing accommodations also require the student to take the responsibility to notify their professor a week ahead of the test that they need to take the test at the learning center. It is not an automatic service. Private tutors in various subjects can also be arranged, usually through the learning center. It's wise to get acquainted with the learning center on day one, if only to see what services are available.

You should also note that every college makes its own decision regarding granting testing accommodations. Their standard for granting such accommodations often varies from school to school. If you have had a 504 plan or an IEP in high school this does not automatically mean you will be granted a 504 plan at college. Most colleges require a complete testing battery for the ADD student that has been given within the past three years. Test data alone is not a guarantee. Each college has a policy for applying for such accommodations, with different levels of deficits needed to qualify for accommodations. Familiarize yourself with their rules on this subject well before day one. In fact, your decision to enroll may be determined by this issue.

Reader Question: What if my child doesn't want to "stand-out." He seems to have done okay in high school with minimal accommodations. Should I push the learning center idea?

The quick answer is yes. You and your child have a lot riding on this financially and emotionally. Would you drive a car without insurance? Think of the learning center as your insurance. At least investigate what is out there for him or her. It would be best if they had a meeting with someone from that office to talk about how they can help students with ADD, "if needed." They will be more likely to seek the help after they have met some staff and looked the place over. How far you push depends on a few factors such as the severity of the ADD, the degree that accommodations were needed in high school, your child's ability to quickly identify and manage problems, and even the degree of difficulty your child might face that semester.

Don't forget, you don't have to actually use the accommodations. Many ADD children at college use the accommodations selectively, depending on the subject and type of test. They can also leave in the usual allotted time, and not use the extended time if they don't need it. Sometimes it is just reassuring to know they have plenty of time; they may not actually need it. Sometimes, the "quiet area" accommodation is the main help and the extra time may not be needed. It is often true too that just having an extra ten minutes can make a big difference.

If your young adult ADD child is living and working, either from your home or in their own apartment, they too need exercise and routine. A job tends to provide that routine, but there still is plenty of free time that should not be wasted. ADD adults are better off directing their attention and energies to learning new skills and developing interests than they are hanging out with peers at a bar.

Step 6: Overcoming disasters – plan redemption

I don't want to dwell on disasters, but they do happen in spite of the best planning. Any young adult can fail, not just young adults with ADD. These ADD adults are at a bit higher risk, but that added risk is likely to be negligible if you and your ADD child have worked together over the years and you have mastered many challenges. The risk factor is likely to be higher if your young adult child is not managing the ADD well, e.g., not taking needed medication, not using student services, etc. Still, even if they are following good ADD management practices, college students can get into a girlfriend or boyfriend crisis, or get into drugs, drinking too much, skipping classes, or even getting sick for a few weeks.

There is always a reset. Assure your young adult child of this fact, no matter what the crisis. Likely there will have to be a pullback of some sorts. You can't manage a crisis of any great degree from a distance, or in a few days. Remember the school calendar at college blitzes by. You may have to get deferred grades in some classes or withdraw altogether. Most schools will allow a medical leave of absence, and will consider readmission, though you likely will have to apply for reinstatement and demonstrate readiness to return.

Disasters can occur outside of college too. A job may be threatened or lost due to problems at work. Financial management may be a disaster with big bills that can't be paid. Mental health and alcohol or drug issues can happen to anyone, including ADD young adults. You can take a similar attitude. Redemption is possible. You can lend a helping hand, but be sure it's not a blank check. There needs to be some serious discussions about how this disaster happened and how it can be prevented.

Step 7: Encourage seeking outside support and direction as an adult

This might be a good time to encourage building a safety net. There are many people out there that can be helpful. As a child and adolescent, the safety net is largely set by parents and school staff. For young adults, this needs to be established by themselves.

Counseling can be very helpful, particularly if the professional involved has experience working with ADD children and adults. Parents should encourage seeking advice and support from a variety of sources. All colleges have counseling and career resources facilities. That may include counselors to help with ADD or learning disability issues specifically. A physician can be consulted about medication options. Fitness centers can offer personal training to help with general health concerns.

Reader Question: How about the accommodations that a young adult person had when he was a child? How can he expect such accommodations in the work place?

Good point there. I generally advise young adults to never use the term "ADD" with peers or supervisors in the work place. They need to simply state, "I work best when…." or "It would help me if…." You are asking for modest changes in working conditions, distribution of work or assistance without referencing "disabilities." If you need more time, or if you need to take notes, chalk it up to being "careful" or "wanting to make sure I got it, because I know this is important." There may be some jobs or some work places that simply won't work out for your child. They need to accept that too. However, most employers are happy to have hard working employees who are "careful."

Step 8: Paint a Positive Long Term Picture

Many individuals with ADD grow up to be highly successful in their adult years. Encourage your child to have positive, realistic dreams. Imagine, with your child, what it will be like for them at some distant point. Describe how they will use their skills and talents, and even their ADD, to reach their goals. Imagine a specific and positive scene. Paint a picture of work, family, hobbies and interests that fit their personality and skills. Revisit this positive place frequently.

Even if your child is now struggling, point to these struggles as a time of testing that will strengthen them for the future. Point to some of the coping strategies noted in this book as tools you see them using in their adult years. Paint a picture of your child proactively seeking assistance in managing their life when needed, while also striving to overcome or minimize the negative effects of ADD. Most importantly, point to their small, recent victories as signs of strength and determination that will carry them to a successful future. Even older children can't get enough praise and encouragement. Remember, you are the coach and the cheerleader!

Age appropriate collaboration

Younger children don't have much of a long-term perspective. Their future vision may be a fantasy. They may see themselves as a sports star or a rock star. They may have a realistic vision too, such as becoming a doctor, architect or engineer. They may think this vision will happen automatically without planning or work on their part. Older children with ADD often don't want to see into the future. They see trouble ahead.

Parents need to accept the young child's vision and they need to help their child see the path ahead. Parents need to help older children face their future with hope and determination. They need to help their child outline a path to success that may be a bit winding and different. Parents need to help both younger and older children see that there are helping forces out there to help then along in their adult years, not just in school. Children of all ages need to hear the stories of many successful professionals who have ADD and who have thrived.

Question: ADD in adults:

    a. Can continue to impair learning and work
    b. Often can be treated with medication and counseling, as with children
    c. Can be managed at college with support services and accommodations
    d. Can be helped by having routine and exercise
    e. All of the above

ABOUT THE AUTHOR

Dr. Schofield has had 35 years of experience with testing and treating ADD in children and adults. Over the past decade his practice has been exclusively in the evaluation and treatment of attention and learning problems.

His education includes a BA with honors in psychology from Clark University in Worcester, Massachusetts and a master's degree and doctorate degree from Michigan State University, East Lansing, Michigan in clinical psychology. Dr. Schofield was inducted into the National Honor Society for psychology (Psi Chi). He completed an American Psychological Association approved one year full-time internship at the Astor Home for Children, Rhinebeck, New York.

Prior to private practice, he worked as Chief Psychologist, Hobart and William Smith College counseling center, Geneva, New York and Chief Psychologist at Clifton Springs Hospital and Clinic, Clifton Springs, New York. The major part of his career over the past 25 plus years has been working in full-time private practice, primarily providing ADD testing and treatment services.

Dr. Schofield has privileges at F.F. Thompson Hospital in Canandaigua, New York and Strong Memorial Hospital, Rochester, New York. He is currently a Clinical Assistant Professor of Psychology in the Psychiatry Department at the University of Rochester Medical School.

Dr. Leon Schofield

More information about Dr. Schofield and more information about the diagnosis and treatment of ADD in children and adults can be found at his website: **www.addexpert.net**.

www.ingramcontent.com/pod-product-compliance
Lightning Source LLC
Chambersburg PA
CBHW062202280526
45788CB00001B/409